RUM, SODOMY
and
THE LASH

A Devon Lad's Life
in Nelson's Navy

Anthony Blackmore

With best wishes.

Anthony Blackmore

June '04

First published in 2002 by the author:

E. A. Blackmore
Covey House
Upper Dunsforth
YORK   YO26 9RU

ISBN   0 9543674 0 5

Set in Garamond 11pt/13.2
and Caslon Open Face

Typeset and printed by David Brown, Maynards Green, Sussex 01435 812506

FOREWORD

I was very glad to hear that Anthony Blackmore was writing a book about his distant relative Samuel Blackmore's life in Nelson's navy, and am delighted to learn that The Nelson Society were instrumental in giving him the pointer that enabled him to make a start on his project.

With nothing for Anthony to go on, other than family tradition, the vital clue was that Samuel was said to have received a medal. One of my colleagues pointed out that this would almost certainly have been the Naval General Service Roll Medal. Reference to the Medal Roll revealed him and one of the ships he had been on.

The author makes no apologies for employing as his main title Churchill's famous thunderous description of the Georgian navy, which was probably the progenitor of the myth created by such films as Charles Laughton's 'Mutiny on the Bounty'. He makes no claim to be an academic historian; thus you will not find the normal PRO citations for his quotations and references. Yet the tale that he tells will delight all devotees, like myself, of the era; and it is refreshing to get a 'lower deck' view of life on board a ship in Nelson's navy especially as Samuel was in the thick of the action, and was taken by the French along with his shipmates in HMS *Berwick* off Corsica. The author's description of the total dismasting of the *Berwick* and her subsequent jury-rigging is replete with technical detail, for which the author is to be congratulated. He rightly acknowledges the assistance given by Peter Goodwin, Keeper and Curator of HMS *Victory*.

The story of Samuel Blackmore makes for enthralling reading. He was a sailor in the Napoleonic Wars (or, more properly, the French Revolutionary War) from 1793 to 1802. Thanks to the notorious press-gang, he spent the first eighteen months in His Majesty's Royal Navy as an 'Able' seaman on board two 'ships of the line', followed by a spell as a prisoner of war in a French prison. On release, he had the good fortune to be drafted into a recently captured, brand-new French frigate *la Minerve*, and spent the next six years and more on her, becoming her coxswain. For nearly all the time he served on *la Minerve*, George Cockburn (a personal friend and protégé of Nelson) was her captain; Cockburn later became famous for burning the White House in the War of 1812.

The prize-money Samuel earned whilst on *la Minerve* meant that, after the "Great War" (as they called the war against Napoleon) was over, he was able to buy his own house, have a servant, and become a Freeman of the City of Dover.

In researching his subject and writing this book, which he has so obviously enjoyed doing, Anthony Blackmore has ferreted out a whole wealth of original sources to support his story. It is particularly refreshing that this book is about the life of a lower deck sailor, and the life he and his shipmates led, rather than about famous admirals and ships of the line. I only wish that Samuel had left us some hitherto unpublished letters or a diary that would shed some new light on the navy of his day as experienced by the 'ordinary people'.

But to revert to the book's title and Churchill's quotation about naval tradition; does it fairly portray life in the Royal Navy during the Napoleonic Wars? Was life on board a King's Ship so terribly brutal as Churchill would have us believe? Strong discipline there was – as ships' logs attest – and it had to be so for the safety of the ship and all on her. It was conditions, not discipline, which led to the mutinies at Spithead and the Nore in 1797. There were bad commanders and good, bad officers and good, in the Royal Navy in Nelson's day.

Alcohol on board ship, as on dry land, formed a necessary part of a man's daily calorie intake, and was frequently used as a substitute for tainted drinking water. Punishment inevitably followed infractions of discipline. Certainly this book in no way looks at the issue of sodomy which will be the province of other writers. I hope that it will help to establish that, at least in the ships that Samuel served on, Churchill gives us a view of life at sea in the Royal Navy during that period which was far from correct.

I wish this book the success it deserves.

VICTOR SHARMAN

Chairman,

The Nelson Society

ACKNOWLEDGEMENTS

First, my sincere thanks to all the many friends whose comments, encouragement and advice have helped me to write this book, and to those who goaded me and spurred me back into action at a time when I had lost momentum. I must especially mention Sue Simpson (then the Secretary of the Nelson Society), Peter Goodwin (Keeper and Curator, HMS *Victory*) and 'Harry' Harrison (of the HMS *Trincomalee* Trust) who had read earlier drafts of the book and urged me to press on with the project, and Helier Hibbs and Jane Ingham for their help in reading the final draft of this book and pointing out masses of 'typos', spelling mistakes, schoolboy howlers and other inaccuracies.

Secondly, I must express my gratitude to The Nelson Society who pointed out that if (as Blackmore family tradition had it) Samuel Blackmore had indeed won a medal, the probability was that his name would feature in the Naval General Service Medal Roll. It did, along with that of his ship, so I was able to piece together his naval career. I am also most grateful to Robert Gardiner of Chatham Press, the acknowledged expert on frigates of the period, who kindly helped me with *la Minerve's* design details, and to the present owner of Samuel's Naval General Service medal for kindly sending me copies of the 1994 auction sale catalogue and the research notes of Capt K J Douglas-Morris.

I am sincerely grateful also to John C Dann, Director of the Clements Library, University of Michigan, who has kindly given me permission to quote so liberally from 'The Nagle Journal' edited by him. This is a magnificent book which vividly portrays life on the lower deck in Nelson's navy.

In connection with the illustrations, my heartfelt thanks are due to Commander Geoff Hunt R.N., whose beautiful miniature '*La Minerve*, off Toulon' hangs in pride of place on my sitting room wall and is reproduced here in colour, and to Sue Simpson for her two 'By God I'll not lose Hardy; back the Mizzen Topsail' drawings. I am also grateful to the West Dumbartonshire Libraries and Museums Service for the picture of the side lever engine by Napier from the paddle steamer *Leven*, to my distant cousin Leslie Simpson for sending me a print of his picture 'The Dover Mail Coach' and to the 'In & Out' Club and their Secretary for allowing me to copy two 19th century prints (the siege of

Toulon in 1793 and the capture by HMS *Dido* of *la Minerve* in 1795) hanging in the Members' Bar.

Finally, my thanks to all the many individuals in countless organisations, up and down the country, whose patient assistance to an elderly amateur historian has made researching this book such an enjoyable experience. I would expressly thank everyone who helped me at the Public Record Office at Kew, the British Library (both at London and at Wetherby), the British Library Newspaper Library at Colindale, the Guildhall Library, London, the Westminster Reference Library, the Post Office (now known as Consignia and shortly, I believe, to be called the Royal Mail) Archives Department at Mount Pleasant, London, the Library of the National Maritime Museum at Greenwich and the Plans Department at Woolwich, and the public libraries, family history units and record offices at Exeter, Exmouth, Dover, Harrogate, Kent, Leeds and Portsmouth. Indeed, I have received so much help from so many organisations and individuals that I am in danger of forgetting to name some of them. If there are others who have helped me, and whose records I quote without thanking them and acknowledging their assistance, will they please forgive me?

Let me end with a 'plug' – by expressing my admiration for all the hard work and skill that has gone into HMS *Trincomalee*. For the benefit of those who do not know (dare I say it – mainly southerners!) she is an 1817 frigate of the *Leda* class, similar in so many ways to HMS *la Minerve*, now happily fully restored and afloat at Hartlepool. No serious naval history student of the period should miss an opportunity to pay her a visit.

ANTHONY BLACKMORE

"I don't say the French can't come. I say they can't come by sea."

Earl St Vincent (formerly Admiral Jervis), First Sea Lord,
speaking in the House of Lords on Napoleon's threatened invasion of England.

INTRODUCTION

Putting together what I knew of our family history as a retirement project, I found that one piece of the jigsaw was missing. My central character, Henry Blackmore (my grandfather's grandfather) was an impoverished tailor who had quit Devon in the depression that followed the Napoleonic War to became a fashionable naval and military tailor in Victorian London. He helped his son-in-law Arthur Liberty to found his famous shop in Regent Street, putting up all but a few hundred pounds of the finance. For more than 150 unbroken years Henry's family, smiths and plumbers, were Parish Clerks at Littleham (now part of Exmouth) in Devon where Henry's father, John, had improved his social status by marrying the vicar's granddaughter.

Newspaper reports showed that two of Henry's relatives joined the Exmouth Volunteers and, later, a cousin joined the Volunteer Rifles, became their crack rifle shot and rose to colour sergeant, but was dismissed at Court Martial for insubordination! I even found a harrowing account of Henry's four year old cousin's agonising death trying to swallow the steam from a boiling kettle.

But all I knew for certain about Henry's sailor uncle, Samuel Blackmore, was that he had been baptised at Littleham in 1777. The rest was family tradition, passed down by Emma Liberty (Henry's daughter) to my grandfather and, by him, to me.

Samuel was said to have been a sailor 'on the lower deck' on HMS *Victory* at Trafalgar (we soon found that was wrong) and to have gained a medal. Cadiz also featured somehow in the story, but no one knew how. The French had captured him, possibly during a raid at Toulon and, on being released after many years as a prisoner of war, they had returned his medals. They had also given him a seal of the City of Calais but why, or what this was, we did not know.

Samuel was said to have gone on to become the captain of a cross Channel packet boat. My grandfather added enigmatically in a note that he was in the habit of going up onto the bridge 'clad as to his feet in carpet slippers.'

You can trace an officer from the Navy Lists but, unless you know what ship a common seaman was on, it is virtually impossible to trace him. However I was sure there was a story somewhere, if only I could find it.

My grandfather's reference to a naval raid seemed to be a possible starting point, but proved not to be – there were numerous raids on France and French held soil during the so-called Napoleonic Wars. These became known as 'the Great War', a title that lasted until the Kaiser started something even bigger in 1914. Strictly speaking there were two wars. The first started (so far as Great Britain was concerned) after the French Revolution with the 'Revolutionary War', when France declared war on her in February 1793. There was one short interlude after the Peace of Amiens in 1802, followed by what is correctly called the 'Napoleonic War' from 1803 until the Battle of Waterloo in 1815.

I next tried to find out about prisoners taken at the siege of Toulon in 1793 but this, too, soon proved to be a dead end as neither side kept proper records of prisoners, and few records have survived. The vital clue was my grandfather's reference to a medal, as I was able to find Samuel, and the ship he was on, in the Naval General Service Medal roll. So, with much sleuthing on my part and help and advice from others, and with endless luck, I was able to piece together Samuel Blackmore's story. Here it is.

And the title to this book? When Winston Churchill was First Lord of the Admiralty before the outbreak of the 1914-18 war, he was told that one of his proposals was contrary to naval tradition. 'Don't talk to me about naval tradition,' he replied, 'it's nothing but rum, sodomy and the lash'.[1]

ANTHONY BLACKMORE   July 2002

---

[1] The precise quotation seems to cause confusion. *The Concise Oxford Dictionary of Quotations* gives it as above, quoting Sir Peter Gretton. *The Oxford Dictionary of Phrase, Saying & Quotation*, under 'The Armed Forces', says;
     "'Naval tradition? Monstrous. Nothing but rum, sodomy, prayers, and the lash."
         Often quoted as "Rum, sodomy and the lash", as in Peter Gretton (1968) Former Naval Person.
     Harold Nicholson: *Diaries and Letters 1945-62* (1968) diary 17 August 1950.'

*To all my fellow bowel cancer victims worldwide,
and to the 34,000, who, in the UK alone, will
join our ranks during the next twelve months.*

x

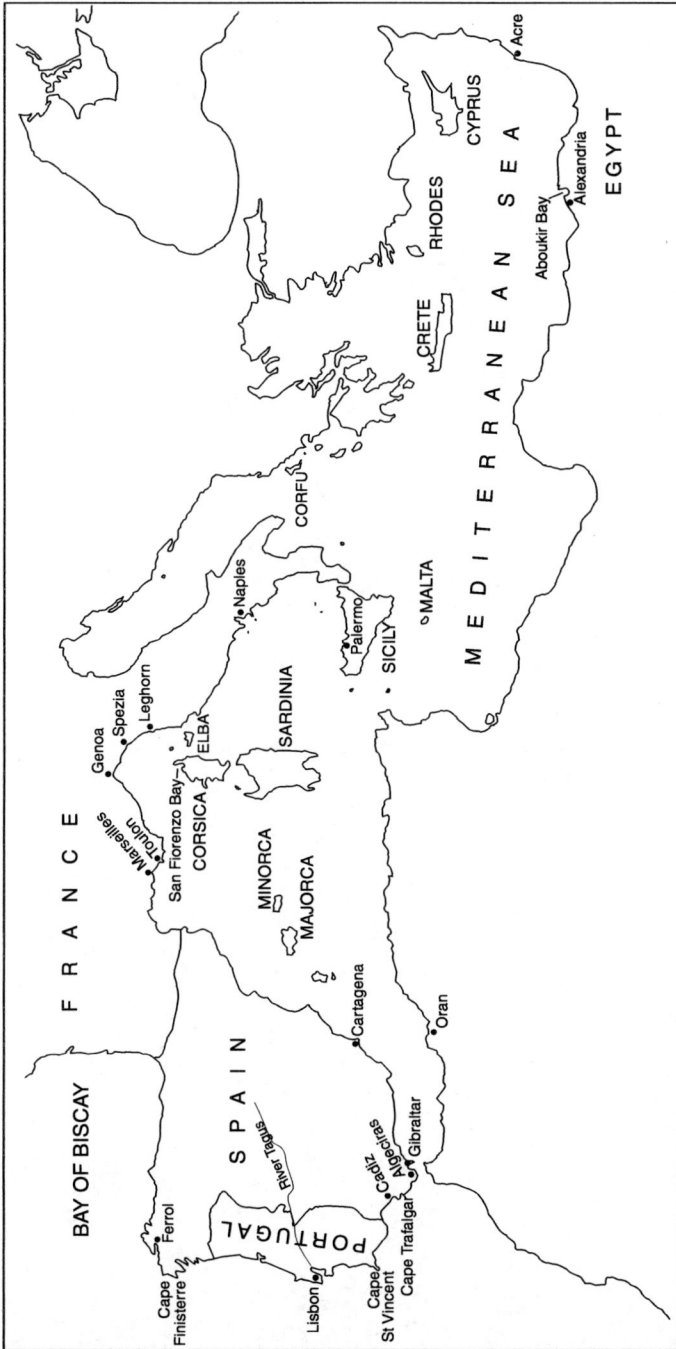

Map of the Mediterranean

LIST OF ILLUSTRATIONS

Map of the Mediterranean   x-xi

HMS la Minerve off Toulon   opp 1

"Destruction of the French Fleet at Toulon, Decr 10th 1793"   opp 10

"The Capture of la Minerve, June 14th 1795"   opp 10

"GOVER'S New Improved Gun Carriage"   36-7

"Interieure de la batterie d'une Frigate"   48

"Engagement between Minerve and Sabina"   52

Samuel Blackmore's Naval General Service medal, with three clasps   56

"By God I'll not lose Hardy; back the mizzen topsail"   78

"Admiral Nelson receiving the Spanish Admiral's sword on board
     the San Josef"   80

Hardy's Monument   104

H.M. Frigate 'MINERVE'   117

Side-lever engine by Napier from the paddle steamer 'Leven'   142

"The Elfin" despatch steamer   145

A side-lever engine.   146

"The London to Paris Mail Coach, at the High Street Canterbury
     Stage, Christmas 1830"   151

Lady Nelson's grave at Littleham   153

HMS la Minerve off Toulon,
by Commander Geoff Hunt, R.N.

CHAPTER 1

On 30 June 1793, two fully laden East Indiamen were heading home and had been battling against an impossible easterly gale which prevented them from making any way up Channel. Samuel Blackmore was on one of them, the *Imperial*.[2] Abandoning the attempt, they were both finally forced to run for shelter in Cork harbour.

Their pleasure and feelings of relief on reaching the safety of the harbour were short-lived. Alas, already sheltering there was a British man-of-war, HMS *Diadem*, of 64 guns and a nominal complement of 525 men. But she was badly under strength. Her captain could hardly believe his luck, as skilled men were hard to come by and men trained on an East Indiaman were, he knew, trained properly. So he put an armed party of stout seamen on board under a lieutenant. He, acting under the authority of his press warrant, took the pick of her crew, 21 young men who had all had, at the very least, the experience of a voyage out to the Far East and back.

This left *Imperial* with barely enough men to sail her, even in fine weather, for the rest of her journey up Channel. The ships of 'John Company', as the Honourable East India Company was known, were a fertile recruiting ground for His Majesty's ships of war. Sometimes, usually far up Channel, the Press Service would strip every single man off an East Indiaman, putting their own skeleton crew of trusted men on board her to bring her back to London, and from where they could be relied upon to find their own way back to the Press Service vessel to which they belonged.

Like many others before him and since, Samuel and his John Company shipmates were faced with an easy choice. Why resist the pressmen, and join *Diadem* as 'prest men' (thereby making themselves marked men, targets for every jumped-up petty officer's 'start') when, by recognising the inevitable, they could enter her with pride as 'volunteers' and thus claim the £5 King's Bounty? Besides, the Royal Navy saw to it that they were properly paid up to date by the ship they were leaving, so there was nothing to lose. It is hardly surprising, therefore, that Samuel and his 20 shipmates all 'volunteered'. The arrangement

---

2 According to the 1994 auction sale catalogue and research notes of Capt K J Douglas-Morris (see Chapter 9).

suited *Diadem's* captain equally well as, if all the men 'volunteered', there could be no possible questions from an offended John Company, let alone difficulties with the Admiralty or his commanding officer. It was his duty to man his ship as best he could and, as the saying goes, it is an ill wind that blows nobody any good.

On board HMS *Diadem*, Samuel and his former John Company shipmates were, later that same day, duly signed on and received their volunteers' bounty, out of which 13s. [65p] was deducted for their hammocks and bedding. The gale slackened and *Diadem* sailed, leaving the unhappy *Imperial* to wait until the gale had finally blown itself out. Even then she was barely able to raise her own anchors, although her remaining crew (elderly men and 'landsmen', most of them) were given every possible encouragement as they sweated at her capstan-bars. There was little her master could do to lighten their burden, apart from waiting until the evening when the wind dropped away. By then *Diadem* was far over the horizon.

Samuel had been looking forward to returning to Exmouth to see his family again. His regret at not seeing them was no doubt profound, but sailors accepted that one of the perils of the sea was the Navy, and its voracious appetite for men. There were compensations. Surprisingly, the sheer weight of hard physical work in a merchant ship could be far worse than in a naval ship where, even though the discipline may have been more severe, there were actually far more men for routine sail-handling and other tasks than in a merchantman. This was because it was the number of guns, and the number of men needed to serve them, that determined the manning level in a King's Ship, and not the number of men needed to handle her sails.

The pay was the problem. Even in times of peace a merchantman's wages were better than in the navy, but in wartime the merchantmen, because of the dearth of trained and experienced sailors, paid as much as three times the antiquated naval wages.

Press-gangs were not supposed to take boys under 18, particularly at that early stage in the war. Even though Samuel had obviously followed 'the trade of the sea' (the one thing that made a man eligible for their attention) for some time when the press men took him, he was still only just 17 and therefore, technically, exempt. But the point was largely academic. He was now on board a King's Ship, one of His Majesty's 'ships of the line', and such fine points as this did not count for much to a lieutenant whose ship was short of men. Samuel therefore decided that, as they had taken him below the legal age, it would be equally logical for him to declare his age as 18 in order to qualify for a full man's wages.

On entering *Diadem* that June day Samuel Blackmore was rated 'Able Bodied' seaman; not bad for a boy just turned 17. It means he already had at least two and probably three or more years experience under his belt in order (literally) to 'learn the ropes' – otherwise he would have been rated 'ordinary seaman' or even 'landsman'. He may even have begun his seafaring career when a young boy, perhaps running away to sea and causing his parents endless worry. Starting as a boy, Samuel would have been assigned to the top-gallant sails at the very top of the mast – simply because the yards and sails up there were lighter for a boy to handle.

Unfortunately the earlier records are missing or incomplete. *Diadem's* muster book says he was 'late of the *Kite* and *Brazen* cutters'. He did not claim to have served in them when applying for a pension (see below). That may have been because he was only a boy at the time and his under-age service would not have counted, but he does not feature in their muster books. *Diadem's* muster book also says he joined her 'from the *Maria* tender'. Tenders were normally used for 'prest men', to house them temporarily and take them out to the ships to which they had been allocated. They were sometimes used for volunteers too, but the reference to a tender may be taken to confirm that Samuel's noble, patriotic act of 'volunteering' was something that only happened once he was firmly on board *Diadem* and realised that there was no worth-while alternative.

In August 1793 Admiral Lord Hood persuaded the citizens of Toulon to declare for the Royalists' cause, and to open their harbour to the English fleet. This was rather surprising, as there had only recently been a similar loyalist rising at Marseilles, just along the coast, which had been put down swiftly and ruthlessly. The loyalists would have been all too well aware of this and must also have known that, although the British and their allies had an impressive fleet, they had only a few soldiers and no proper army there to support them.

The Convention straight away declared Toulon 'hors la loi' and the army of the Republic laid siege to it. Not all were as enthusiastic for the royalists as the city fathers, however. The French sailors, in particular, were reluctant to hand their ships over to the Royal Navy. On entering Toulon, Lord Hood;

> 'Sent notice to Rear Admiral St. Julien, a turbulent spirit, to whom the seamen had given command of the French fleet to procede without delay into the inner harbour and put their powder on shore, and those that did not would be treated as enemies'.

Hood landed 1,500 men 'to take possession of the forts which commanded the ships in the Road.'[3] St Julien, however, escaped during the night with seven line-of-battle ships 'which were principally attached to him'. Even the remaining French ships and men were a worry; Hood had 'apprehensions of some desperate attempt being made within, by upwards of 5,000 disaffected seamen', and therefore;

> 'judged it expedient to embark them in four of the most unserviceable ships … totally dismantled of their guns except two on the forecastle for signals in case of distress; they had no small arms and only 20 cartridges on board of each, and sailed as flags of truce; two for Brest, one for Rochfort and one for l'Orient'.[4]

Diadem's lines[5] show her to be an extremely short, tubby '64', very broad in the beam, rated as a 'third rate'. She was, no doubt, useful in a blow, and in rough weather her wide beam meant that her lower deck gun ports would have been less exposed to the waves than those of a narrower ship, but no wonder Nelson later compared her sailing qualities unfavourably with those of his own beloved *Agamemnon*.

Diadem, part of the Mediterranean Fleet, was said to have been one of the ships that sailed with Hood into Toulon harbour. A reference to the captain's log, however, shows that she had been employed that summer cruising from Spithead to Cork and back, remaining at Spithead from 14 July until 12 August. During the whole of this period she 'exercised the Great Guns and small arms' practically every Tuesday and Friday, even when riding at anchor at Spithead.

She did not, in fact, depart for the Mediterranean until September, when she sailed southwards escorting a convoy. She passed Gibraltar on 9 November and dropped her convoy off at Minorca, heading north and 'Working into Toulon' (according to her log) on 19 November. When she arrived next day in Toulon Harbour, she;

> 'Found riding here HM Ships *Victory*, Lord Hood, *Britannia*, Vice Adm[l] Hotham … with several Line of Battle Ships & Frigates also Spanish Fleet; with several French Line of Battle Ships & Frigates… Wash'd Lower Gun Deck'.

Diadem's two months or so at Toulon were mostly passed 'Rowing Guard'. Entries in the captain's log show that she herself was not involved in the bombardment;

---

3   'Toulon Papers', Naval Chronicle, vol II, p26
4   'Toulon Papers', Naval Chronicle, vol II, p26
5   Plans can be seen at the Woolwich plans department of the National Maritime Museum Library at Greenwich.

'Disembarked our Soldiers … arrived HM Ship *Vulcan*… Fresh Gales, hard Rain. Arrived *Conflagration* fire ship with her head and Bowsprit gone. Heavy fire from the Batterys [sic] On Shore… At 6AM unmoor'd and Shifted our Birth … constant firing at Shore… Obs^d very heavy firing of Great Guns & Musquetry near Fort [Malbousquet] … punish'd Wm Burns (Seaman) with I doz^n for Neglect… Launch disembarking troops… Rec'd fresh Beef. Punish'd Jas. [?Tanel] (Seaman) with I doz. for Dirt & Drunkene*ſs*.'

With his hammock slung on the lower gun deck, going up to the 'heads' on the exposed bow of the deck above in order to answer a call of nature did not seem an attractive proposition to a drunken sailor on a cold, stormy night so, like others both before and after him, William Burns was probably guilty of relieving himself down into the hold! The log continues;

'Sent 200; 24pd shot to Cape Sepat Battery; rowed guard … 7AM the Ad^l made the signal for Launches unarm'd sent all our Boats to A*ſs*ist in Towing a Floating Battery into the Mole … sent 100-24pound Shot to Fort Mulgrave … Launch Disembarking Troops from *Romulus*'.

On 12 December they were ordered to prepare for sea and 'bent on' a new mainsail received from the French sail loft, but it was too big so her sailmakers spent the day reducing its size. Next day they sailed for Leghorn. From then until the end of February they were cruising up to Genoa and back to Leghorn, where *Diadem* 'Rec'd 2 Armourers one from *Berwick* & one from *Terrible* to a*ſs*ist in Repairing the Boilers'.[6]

Nelson had been on half pay for six years, but had just been recalled and given command of *Agamemnon* (64 guns) at Toulon; 'Eggs & Bacon' to her crew. It was not until five years later, after the Battle of the Nile, that he fell for Lady Emma Hamilton's charms, but he first met her in 1793 when, having the fastest 'ship of the line' in the fleet, he was sent from Toulon with despatches for Naples where her husband was the British Ambassador. Nelson's mission was to persuade the King of Naples to send troops to help defend Toulon, where one third of *Agamemnon's* crew had been left behind on shore to help in the fighting. He was successful, as a contingent of Neapolitan troops joined the allies. Sir William Hamilton (aged 63) had recently married Emma (then 27), until then the mistress of his nephew Charles Greville who had been anxious to rid himself of her. Commending her, Greville had written to his uncle;

'She is the only woman I have ever slept with without having ever had any of my senses offended, & a cleanlier, sweeter bedfellow does not exist.'

---

6 i.e. her galley coppers; she was *not* a steam ship!

A mixed army from various nations manned Toulon's perimeter defences, including Austrians, Sardinians (as well as a small British contingent, at no time more than 2,360 men) and also the Spanish who, at that time, were still their allies. All the sailors and marines from the ships in Hood's fleet that could be spared joined them. So the tradition in the Blackmore family proved to be right; Samuel was, indeed, at Toulon but, as we shall see later, that was not where he was taken prisoner. *Diadem* missed the heat of the battle, but even if she herself was not involved in the fighting, what about Samuel? If *Agamamnon* could afford to leave behind some 200 men to swell the ranks of Hood's naval detachment when Nelson was sent to Naples, surely *Diadem* herself had at least half her men fighting on shore? It is inconceivable that a large number of her men would not have joined the naval detachment. What stories Samuel, in later years, must have had to tell!

At first, the French with some 15,000 troops could make no impression on the defences of Toulon. However, a bright young artillery officer was soon sent by the Revolutionary Command to take charge, called Napoleon Bonaparte, who first made his name by rescuing the situation. One look at the guns showed him that they had not even been properly aimed, as they were all firing far too low. The furnaces for heating cannon balls to near-white heat (lethal on a wooden ship, but often equally dangerous to the gunners who had to fire them) were situated in houses hundreds of yards away from the guns and, as a result, the balls had cooled off before they were fired. Napoleon, whilst;

> 'overlooking the construction of a battery which the enemy endeavoured to interrupt by their fire, called for some person who could write, that he might dictate an order. A young soldier stepped out of the ranks and ... began to write accordingly. A shot from the enemy's battery covered the letter with earth…"Thank you – we shall have no occasion for sand this bout" said the military secretary.'

Napoleon, much impressed with the 'gaiety and courage of the remark' of the young soldier, saw to his advancement. He became the celebrated General Junot, later Duc D'Abrantes.[7]

From the day Napoleon arrived, what had at first seemed to the allies to be a brilliant move against revolutionary France gradually assumed a different perspective. The situation deteriorated daily. The French army, growing every day, increased to as many as 45,000 men, whereas at one stage Hood had

---

[7] 'The Life of Napoleon Buonaparte' by Sir Walter Scott (1827). The family changed its name to Bonaparte in 1796. (Before the invention of blotting paper, dry sand was used.)

received only 800 Sardinians and 2,000 from Naples as reinforcements, which 'served considerably to cheer the spirits of the garrison'. At no time did he have more than 17,000 men to guard the town's 15 mile perimeter.

The marines were in their element but the sailors in the naval detachment felt strange behind muskets, and preferred the cutlass to the bayonet. They were far more at home manning the big naval guns that had been taken out of their ships and mounted in the fortresses overlooking the harbour and the smaller forts and redoubts round about. Unfortunately, however, many of these had been sited and designed with the defence of the harbour from sea-based attacks in mind and were not well placed for defending the ever-shrinking perimeter from landward.

The enemy managed to open a battery of twenty four 24-pounders upon the British gunboats, but they were 'very soon dismounted … and the works totally destroyed, with very great slaughter'. The army authorities in Gibraltar had been asked by Hood to send 1,500 troops. They only sent 750, but the Grand Master of Malta generously sent 1,500. By the beginning of November there was an open rift between Lord Hood ('The Lord', as Nelson used to refer to him in his letters) and Don Langara the Spanish Admiral who thought that he, rather than Hood, should be in charge, and;

> 'began at this time more openly to disclose the treachery, which had been long been concealed under a base hypocrisy more worthy of an Inquisitor General than of a Naval Officer'.

On 15 November a large force of French vigorously attacked Fort Mulgrave, a log-built redoubt which the British had constructed to protect their ships in the harbour;

> 'one of the most essential posts that covered the shipping in the Harbour of Toulon … principally directed against that part which was occupied by the Spaniards on the right'.

The Spaniards retreated, 'firing their muskets in the air' (in other words, without any intention of hitting anyone) but General O'Hara, who had taken over command of the British troops in place of Admiral Hood;

> 'instantly directed a Company of the Royals to advance, who gallantly leapt the Works and put the enemy to flight, after leaving about 600 men dead and wounded in the field. The loss of the English amounted to only 61'.[8]

Young Bonaparte knew that the British would never risk losing their fleet, and

---

[8] Quotations here are from the Naval Chronicle.

7

that this was the key to the whole situation. With the gunner's instinct for concentrating his fire on one place at a time, he captured the outer redoubts that protected the town from landward, one by one, and then Fort Mulgrave itself, one of the two main fortresses that controlled the harbour.

The end, when it came, was both sudden and chaotic. On 17 December 1793 the revolutionary forces (now said to number as many as 120,000 men) launched a simultaneous assault during a storm on all the defences. Each of the different national contingents had a sector of the perimeter to defend but, because of language difficulties, communications between adjoining sectors were often non-existent. Many of the allied troops (but not the British contingent) deserted their posts and ran, leaving the British dangerously exposed.

There had been sporadic firing at the ships in the harbour for some days. Nelson describes sitting on a court martial, with shot and shell whistling overhead. But now the ships came under continuous, heavy and concentrated artillery fire and Hood was forced to order a withdrawal in a hurry. It was only with the greatest difficulty that some of the sailors got back to their ships' boats before it was too late, but the retreat was well managed. *Robust*, Captain the Hon. J K Elphinstone – later Admiral Lord Keith – was the last ship out and, surprisingly, not a single one of the British forces, soldiers, sailors or marines, was captured in the final retreat.

The allies were successful, in all the confusion, in blowing up the store houses, arsenal and magazine and also were able to destroy the fireship *Conflagration* (which was being repaired, and unable to sail) to prevent her falling into French hands. They also managed to sail out four 'ships-of-the-line' and a dozen frigates, but there remained the problem of the others that could not be sailed out in time, and also those still building on the stocks in the naval dockyard. They could not risk any of these falling back into the hands of the French. Hood put Sir Sidney Smith[9] (not, technically, holding a commission in the Navy, and even his knighthood was a foreign one, but with a reputation for acts of daring) in charge of the all-important task of burning them.

His assignment was, in fact, not as simple as it sounds as the French masses, never strongly loyalist, grew daily in revolutionary fervour as the Army of the Republic advanced and the perimeter shrank. There was trouble in gaining access to the naval dockyards which were locked and barred to the allies, with a boom across the entrance. Even the galley-slaves, French convicts condemned to

---

[9] Said by Napoleon to be the man who deprived him of his destiny because of his later exploits in the defence of Acre.

the galleys until they died, were anticipating a better deal if the Revolutionary forces regained control. The noise of hammering as they sought to break off their chains to fight for the advancing Republican Army against the Royalists could be heard even above the ever-nearer gunfire.

Sir Sidney had been assigned a party of Spanish troops to assist him in his vital task, but they panicked and fled, with the result that only nine of the ships were destroyed. Before quitting, they managed to blow up (rather than scuttle, as they had been instructed) a powder ship, and the explosion wrecked one of the British gunboats, killing some of her crew. Shooting, fire, explosions and smoke were everywhere. Another powder ship also blew up in all the confusion, but Smith and his men avoided injury and managed to withdraw to the safety of the British fleet. Vol II of the Naval Chronicle makes good reading;

> 'Sir Sidney Smith and the officers immediately under his orders surrounded by a tremendous conflagration of ships and arsenal, had nearly completed the hazardous services assigned to them, when the loud shouts, and the Republican songs of the approaching enemy were heard at intervals, amidst the bursting of shells and firing of musketry.'

The Spaniards under Smith were now behaving with open hostility. When he found that they had not set fire to any of the ships in the inner basin, as he had ordered them;

> 'he therefore hastened with the Boats under his command towards the basin, that he might endeavour, though at so late a period, to counteract the perfidy of the Spaniards: when lo! to his great mortification, he found that the boom had been laid across, and was obliged to desist in his attempts to cut it, from the repeated vollies of musketry directed towards his boats from the flag ship and the wall of the Royal Battery.'

It was later established by the publication of Robespierre's 'Political Testament' that, as Hood had all along supposed, the French had indeed been in league with Don Langara, the Spanish Admiral, which explains how Smith's mission became almost impossible.[10]

Smith's own report (like Nelson, he was never slow to boost his own image) later in the same volume of the Naval Chronicle is also worth reading. For example, his young midshipman had carefully positioned a fire ship;

> 'the guns … going off on both sides as they heated in the direction that was given them towards those quarters from whence we were most apprehensive of the enemy forcing their way upon us, checked their career;'

---

10 Naval Chronicle, vol II.

Smith and his team were able to escape in the confusion caused by the explosion of the second powder ship as it blew up. But he left behind, intact, what amounted to a whole fleet of ships (ships that, later, were to cause the British endless problems) and several others part built on the stocks. One of these happened to be a sleek new frigate. She was somewhat larger than most British frigates of that period, had fine lines and was to be equipped with 18-pounders – heavier armament than most British frigates then possessed. By the time of her launching ceremony the following year, the French had recently lost to the Royal Navy a frigate called *Minerve*[11] so, in accordance with their normal practice, the new frigate was named *'la Minerve'*…

The British sailors were delighted to be back on board again and infinitely preferred the orderly life they knew so well; watch on, watch off, and duff on Sundays. But, for the citizens of Toulon, and particularly for those who had been royalists, or had even worked for them, whether supporters or not, life was somewhat less rosy. The white fleur-de-lys flags and emblems, the symbols of the royalists, were quickly torn down and replaced with the red white and blue tricoleur. The white royalist hat cockades were replaced by tricoleur cockades, too. But it was too late. In Paris the 'Committee on Public Safety' had already ordered the town to be burnt down and every single royalist to be killed.

There was complete panic and pandemonium. The allies had no alternative but to leave the city and its inhabitants to their fate. The British Navy took off 15,000 loyalists, which was as many as the ships could carry. There was a stampede. Many hundreds, mostly women and children, were drowned as they were pushed over the water's edge or fought for places in the boats. The rest were less lucky. 200 dockyard workers were shot for helping the allies. Crowds were herded together and despatched with grape-shot. A French general bragged that every day, for ten days, 200 heads had fallen to the guillotine. In all, some 6,000 were promptly butchered, but;

> 'Amidst the excesses and cruelty which the French at this time committed, it was their custom to sell the Imperialists who fell into their hands, to the Spaniards, by whom some were transported to the mines in South America, and others selected for recruits.'[12]

---

11 Renamed *San Fiorenzo*, as there was already a frigate called *Minerva* in the Royal Navy; indeed, a whole class of frigates was named after her. There was another frigate of the same name in the Neapolitan navy, and also an East-Indiaman. Minerva was the Roman equivalent of Athena, the Greek goddess of wisdom, war, poetry and the liberal arts.

12 Marshall's Naval Biography, vol I, p 520. It is said that, after the Armada, Spanish prisoners were put to work in the lead mines in North Yorkshire.

"Destruction of the French Fleet at Toulon, Decr 10th 1793"
from Naval Achievements by J. Jenkins, 1816

"The Capture of la Minerve, June 14th 1795"
from Naval Achievements by J. Jenkins, 1816

Nelson saw no excuse for leaving so many French ships unburned when the allies withdrew, and was utterly sickened by the blood-bath that followed; it is said that this, above all else, accounted for his loathing of revolutionary France. Sharing most serving naval officers' prejudice against Sir Sidney Smith because of his over-riding self interest and flair for publicity, and blaming him for the failure to destroy the ships, he wrote;

> 'Lord Hood mistook the man: there is an old saying, "Great talkers do the least, we see."'

This criticism, and a more outspoken one by Nelson's friend Collingwood (who was far away with the Channel Fleet at the time) were less than fair. At Cape St Vincent, for example (hailed as a national victory) the British took just four ships of the line – and two of those were the ones captured by Nelson personally – whereas Sir Sidney Smith, at Toulon, destroyed ten ships of the line and four smaller ships. He would have destroyed many more if the Spaniards under him had come up to scratch. But 18 ships of the line and seven frigates and smaller ships were handed back on a plate to the French. If blame was required for the failure to sail out or destroy more of them, Lord Hood had made no contingency plans. He then entrusted this vital task to the Spanish, who had already proved totally unreliable. It was only at the last moment that he called on Smith to rescue the situation.

Robespierre later confirmed that the French had attacked at the pre-arranged time and the Spanish had duly fled, leaving the flank of the British contingent unprotected. He also stated that the blowing up of the powder ships, rather than sinking them, had been agreed beforehand with the French, but they had intended to sink the British war ships by this means and the ruse had gone wrong.

Sir John Moore realised that, as his regiment, the 51st, was the last to arrive at Gibraltar, it would be the last to leave. He therefore spent several weeks kicking his heels there, knowing that it would be some while before the 51st would be allowed by the timid Governor, Sir Robert Boyd, to leave for Toulon, in spite of Lord Hood's urgent requests for more British troops. At last the 51st were allowed to sail but, by the time they arrived at Toulon, it had fallen. Historians tend to have a favourable view of Lord Hood, because of his well-earned reputation in earlier days and the respect of his contemporaries, but the army, and he, did not see eye to eye. Army officers had, apparently, for long been advising Hood that Toulon was untenable and should be evacuated. Moore wrote in his journal;

'It was evident … that they should be forced to do it soon, perhaps with the loss of the greater part of the troops, and possibly even part of the fleet. This was represented in the strongest manner to Lord Hood, who chose to follow his own opinion.'

In fairness to Lord Hood, he had advocated a strong counter-attack on Fort Mulgrave to retake it, and again pressed this course at the Council of War;

'But his spirited counsel was rejected, and the evacuation resolved upon; which the panic of the foreign troops … would have rendered still more horrible than it proved, but for the steadiness of the British seamen.'[13]

Toulon would have made an ideal naval base but, with the benefit of hindsight, it was realised that it would have been impossible to hold it without a massive army. Besides, the French would have felt obliged to recapture it regardless of cost and, at that distance from home ports, it would have been very difficult to keep an occupying army supplied.

After its hurried exit at Christmas 1793 the Mediterranean Fleet, under Admiral Lord Hood, set about blockading Toulon. This was necessary in order to put a stranglehold on the French economy and, above all, to bottle up the French fleet in Toulon harbour and prevent it from coming out to destroy Britain's commercial shipping. *Diadem* spent her time beating up and down outside Toulon and Hyères, the Giens[14] Peninsular and the islands off Hyères. In the summer the weather was unbearably hot, except when the Mistral blew (a bitingly cold wind that whistles down the Rhône valley from the Alps for four or five days at a time, making life even on dry land unpleasant) and during the winter the gales and the short, heavy seas caused constant damage to the blockading ships.

After the loss of Toulon, Hood's ships could still shelter from storms in Hyères Bay, not far to the east, but they badly needed a proper base where supplies could be safely kept and ships could refit and be repaired. Corsica was a good possibility. The population were loyalists, but the revolutionary French army held the fortresses. So, whilst the rest of the fleet under Hood carried on with the blockade of Toulon, Nelson was sent to Corsica. Working closely with the army, ('The army, as usual, is well dressed and powdered', he reported[15], with the

---

13 Scott, 'The Life of Napoleon Buonaparte'
14 Where, one and a half centuries later (just after the war) the author spent two long summer holidays as a boy with a French family and the local fishermen in their boats. Little did he then know of the events of the 1790s now related.
15 Capt.A.T.Mahan, 'The Life of Lord Nelson, the Embodiment of the Sea Power of Great Britain' [London, 1899] vol I.

Navy's usual regard for the junior service) he led the Navy's contingent in the attack and supplied some of *Agamemnon's* 24-pounder guns for a bombardment. These were man-handled up the cliffs by the sailors, complete with mountings, powder and ammunition, and remounted in proper gun positions. The fortresses were captured, Nelson losing the sight of his eye in the process, and San Fiorenzo (now called St Florent) was established as a base with a safe anchorage.

CHAPTER 2

Corsica was ideally placed for the fleet, whose main task was to watch the French fleet in Toulon and make sure it did not come out. Furthermore, Napoleon had been appointed to command the Revolutionary army in Italy and the land war had moved on. Nice and the Riviera (formerly belonging to Sardinia) and much of the Italian coast had now fallen under French domination. Genoa, nominally neutral, supplied a starving France with corn. Thanks to the totally inadequate roads,[16] the only way these badly needed supplies could reach their destination, and the only supply route for Napoleon's army in Italy, was by sea – and here the British were masters.

Hood was personally involved in the assault on Corsica and, when not himself blockading Toulon, left his second-in-command, Vice Admiral Hotham, there to manage the blockade for him. But Hotham did not apply the same zeal or enthusiasm to his task and, to Nelson's astonishment, let a squadron of the French ships (equal in number to Hotham's own squadron and therefore, in Nelson's eyes, easy meat) slip out of Toulon under his very nose. He said he believed it was making for Corsica, and thought it better to run there to join the rest of Hood's fleet which, then having superior numbers, would easily defeat it. But the French did not show up at Corsica and had vanished, posing a serious threat.

After its capture, Corsica became a British dependency under Sir Gilbert Elliot as Governor General, but administered by the Corsicans. The loss of the island was a serious blow to the French, who promised to eat their New Year's dinner there. It was known that a large fleet of transports was readying itself in Toulon to carry the Revolutionary army to Corsica.

On 7 July 1794, a year after joining *Diadem,* Samuel was transferred to another 'third rate', HMS *Berwick*, a ship of 74 guns and 625 men, built in 1775. Life on *Berwick* carried on much as it did on *Diadem* after the fall of Toulon – blockade duty off Toulon, bombarding French defences on Corsica and harrying French and Genoese coastal shipping.

Berwick was thought to be a good design, as the notes on her plans at Woolwich

---

16 'The miserable Corniche Road could not have sufficed as the sole line of communications for forty thousand troops.' Mahan.

indicate that East India Company ordered another like her in 1779 and the Navy ordered two more to the same design in 1780. However, whatever may have been the view in Whitehall of *Berwick's* sterling qualities, they were not shared by those who had the doubtful privilege of sailing in her. J.A. Gardner, who served as a midshipman in her from 1794 to 1795 and was there with Samuel Blackmore for two months in 1795, wrote;[17]

'In July [1793] while cruizing off Toulon the fleet encountered a tremendous gale, and the old *Berwick*, who always bore the name of a bad sea boat, proved it on this occasion with a vengeance. First the bowsprit went, about two feet from the outer gammoning; bore up, and got the runners and tackles forward to secure the foremast. At daylight made the signal of distress... The rigging being new, it became so slack that we were obliged to set it up, with a very heavy sea running, which was done in a seaman-like manner; but mark what follows. After the lower rigging was set up, and while before the wind, the main sail, of all the sails in the world, was set, and the ship hove to slap at once, by which she was nearly thrown on her beam ends. The main yard went in the slings, and the main topmast and half the main top carried away, the foremast sprung in two places, and the mizzen mast in three; of the main-top men of one watch, seventeen in number, one was killed, another drowned and several of the others severely hurt, but by falling on the splinter netting were fortunately saved. The wreck of the main yard had nearly knocked two ports into one on the main deck, while that of the main topmast got under the counter, damaged the copper and almost unshipped the rudder before it could be cleared... It is a fact that the ship rolled sixteen or eighteen feet of her foreyard in the water, and laboured so dreadfully that on our arrival in port the oakum was found to have worked so much out of the seams ... that it was astonishing that we succeeded in reaching Gibraltar... I do not mean to throw the blame on anyone, but I cannot help thinking that the ship was somehow or other badly handled, to say nothing of her being a bad sea boat.'

Lord Hood, to Nelson's great regret, was recalled and sailed for England on 11 October 1794. Worse, he was succeeded by Vice Admiral Hotham. In the light of subsequent events, it is ironic to note one entry made in *Berwick's* log whilst she was in Leghorn Road, soon after Samuel joined her;

'Saturday 24th July 1794; Joined Co. with the Fleet and hove too [sic] at ½ past 5 filled and made sail at 6 Cheered Adm¹ Hotham...'

The account in 'James' of events towards the end of 1794 and in the spring of 1795 differs somewhat from the version given in the log. It is therefore necessary

---

17 'Above and Under Hatches', by J.A.Gardner, 1906, now reprinted by Chatham Publishing.

to reconstruct *Berwick*'s story by picking one's way between the two accounts with care.

Captain Sutherland, who had commanded *Diadem* when Samuel was on her, was now in command of *Berwick*. It was either his secretary, or some more junior clerk under his supervision, who was responsible for writing up the 'Captain's Journal' – the official log. He based this on the brief entries in the Master's log, but added any further details requested by Sutherland. As so often happens, great events are eclipsed by details of bullocks slaughtered. Much of the log for 1794 is taken up with the huge discrepancies between the beef and pork stated to be in the casks purchased at Leghorn and their actual contents. Obviously, the Italians had acquired a certain reputation for dishonesty!

The author of the Captain's Journal was not greatly concerned with spelling, but was anxious to give us some idea of what was actually happening on board. Extracts from the captain's log, complete with the original spelling, show that life on a '74' was neither as exciting nor as financially rewarding as life on a frigate;

> 'Saturday 1st November 1794. Light Airs. Washed the Lower Deck & Worked the Ventilators[18]… Parted Company with HM Ship *Agamemnon*. Killed a Bullock… Anchored in Forinza Bay … found here HM Ships *Maleager* [sic] and *Fox* Cutter … saw the *Maleager* bring too a French Gun Boat… 4AM Adm[l] made the *Maleager* Sigl. to Chase ENE & *Tarter* to Chase NBE[19] Scrub'd hammocks

> '31 December 1794 All the Fleet in Company & a Strange Brig Prize to the *Dido* at 9 the *Agamemnon* made the Sig[l] for a strange sail NEBE out 2 Reefs.'

Christmas 1794 and the New Year were spent with the Mediterranean Fleet off Toulon on blockade duty under storm canvas, but the French fleet were snug in their harbour. Nelson wrote to his wife Fanny in January 1795;

> 'We have had nothing but gales of wind, but in *Agamemnon* we mind them not; she is the finest ship I ever sailed in.'

But two weeks later he wrote to Sir William Hamilton, Emma's husband;

> 'We have had the most tremendous weather, such as I have never experienced before in any seas; it blew a perfect hurricane.'

By now, Captain William Smith had taken over from Captain Sutherland and was captain of *Berwick*. Early in January 1795, while Nelson was writing about the frightful weather which the whole fleet had been experiencing, the first note

---

18 This shows that the new theories about keeping a crew healthy by cleanliness and ventilation were being taken seriously in the Mediterranean Fleet.
19 North by East. NEBE means North East by East.

is made in *Berwick's* log which has some bearing on the ominous events that were to follow;

> '...main & futtock shrouds parted, fitted preventer stays[20] – making 5" per hour – and preventer main shrouds.'

On 16 January 1795, the Mediterranean Fleet of 15 'ships of the line', now under the command of Admiral Hotham, was riding at anchor in San Fiorenzo Bay, on the north western coast of Corsica

It must have been just about impossible for the captain's secretary to write up the log neatly at sea in such rough weather as Nelson describes, and there is an enormous ink blob over it. At anchor, however, there is no need to record, hour by hour, the ship's position, course, speed and depth of water. Instead the log, in the same hand but much, much neater, merely says 'Moored in Feorenzo Bay'.

As a result of the recent gales, a heavy cross-swell was rolling into the bay. *Berwick* was repairing her storm damage and had taken down at least some of her topmasts; the log shows that the fore-topgallent mast had not yet been 'struck below'. Her three lower masts, still complete with the fighting 'tops' (the platforms part-way up each mast from where the marines shot at the officers on the decks of opposing ships) had, according to 'James', been stripped of their rigging, but it is clear from the log that this was not entirely accurate.

Now comes the crucial part of the tale;

> 'Sunday 11th January 1795... Opened 1 cask of Pork Contents 50 Pieces; one of Leghorn marked 300 lbs short of weight 54 lbs ... came On Board 3 Carpenters to Survey the Ship, & 3 Masters belonging to *Captain, Egmont & Diadem*, and survey'd 6 Casks of Flower Destroy'd by Ratts [sic] & 3 D°ᶻ of Reasons [sic], found 385 lbs of Flower ate; & condemn'd 557 lbs of -Do- found also 236 lbs of Reasons ate by the Ratts condemn'd 175 lbs of -Do- One cask of Pork weight 300 lbs 6 Beds & 16 outside Jackets... Stripping the Main Mast...
>
> '15th January. Picking Oakum. Caulking Buttocks & setting up Preventer

---

20 A stay is the rope from the top of the mast (or one of the lower sections of a mast) that goes diagonally down to the bows (or to the bowsprit or a lower section of the mast ahead) which holds it upright and takes wind forces from that direction. A preventer stay is a spare stay, usually of somewhat thinner rope, that is tied to the stay itself at intervals by 'snaking'. It is intended to take part of the strain on the stay and, if the stay should part in a blow or be shot away, to act as a temporary stay until the stay itself can be replaced.
'Preventer shrouds' serve the same function for the shrouds - the ropes from the mast down to the 'chains' on the sides of the ship, slightly aft of the mast, that are the main supports for the mast and take most of the force of the wind on the sails.

Shrouds… Got 2 prs of Shrouds to secure the mast… A heavy Swell Setting Into the Bay the Ship Labouring much…

'16th January. Getting Ready 2 Pair of Main Shrouds to secure the Main Mast. The Ship still labouring much… At ½ pst 4 In setting up the Starboard Rigging the Throat Seizings Broak & some of the lanyards the Mast went by the Board. At ¾ Past 4 the Mizen went by the Board, at 5 in Striking the Fore-Topmast the Fore Mast went by the Board. Emp in Clearing the Wreck Fore & Main Topmast Broak and Fore Top Gllᵗ Mast. Cut the End of the Main Yard to clear it of the Sheet Anchor… Sent Launch to secure wreck of the Fore Mast. Lost Sundries Rigging Blocks &c.'

So there we have it. Her main mast (now in the water) had been 'stripped' five days previously, but surely it would have had 'preventer shrouds' fitted? The other two masts, which were either not supported at all or, having regard to the swell, were insufficiently supported, were also rolled over the side. The damage to the ship, especially her decks, must have been considerable, with all three masts being wrenched out of her like this. Her masts were 'stepped' on the keelson, and she was lucky not to have had the bottom ripped out of her as the masts went overboard.

One can imagine the horrifying sequence of events as each of the masts, in turn, went down. First, what supporting rigging there was had snapped at the dead-eyes where the lanyards connected the 'throats' (the lower end of the shrouds) to the 'chains' at the ship's side. The mast, now free of its supports, began to hinge on the 'partners' on the upper deck and, at the same time, the foot of the mast jumped out of the slot into which it was 'stepped' on the keelson. The weight of the mast now gave it momentum as it began to swing over, slowly at first but with increasing speed, tearing through what was left of the partners and ripping through the decks at each level, destroying them like matchwood. At the same time the foot of the heavy mast, now free of its step on the keelson, swung upwards as the mast, hinged around the splintered decking, accelerated towards the horizontal, also ripping upwards through the lower decks. The ship, already heeled to the swell that started the masts in motion, assumed an alarming angle. The mast then crashed through the side of the ship in a tangle of rigging as it went overboard, whilst the foot of the mast wreaked corresponding damage on the other side as it swung upwards.

There was a huge amount of other damage; for example, *Berwick's* wheel was directly ahead of the mizzen mast, the pumps were both adjacent to the mainmast and the galley was by the foremast – these were all wrecked as well.

Nelson seems not to have had a very high opinion of Captain Smith, and wrote to his old friend William Locker[21], Lieutenant-Governor of the Royal Hospital at Greenwich;

'*Agamemnon*, St. Fiorenzo, January 17th, 1795.

My dear Friend… We are a week arrived here from a cruise of three weeks off Toulon, during which time we were fifteen days under storm-staysails, – indeed such a series of bad weather I never experienced; the Ships most of them strained a good deal, but sustained no material damage… We saw three French Frigates, but from the Admiral's anxiety to keep the Fleet together, he did not make the signal for the Frigates to chase them till too late in the day, and they most unluckily escaped… The Admiral is anxious to get to Sea again, to cover our Convoy and expected reinforcements from England, and was only waiting till *Berwick*, commanded by our shipmate Smith, was got ready for Sea; but waiting for her must now be at an end, for last night a very heavy sea rolling into the Gulph, the *Berwick* not having, I understand, her rigging set up, lost all her masts, and is now a most complete wreck. I don't think our shipmate has much improved in the art of seamanship since we parted. The Admiral, as you will believe, is much out of humour with him, thinking we have not a Seventy-four to spare … remember me most kindly to all your family, and believe me ever,

Your most obliged,
HORATIO NELSON.'

The first thing Hotham did, and rightly, was to get rid of Captain Smith;

'Saturday 17th January 1795… Ans^d the Sig^l for a Petty Officer, Launch on Shore … & Came on Board Cap^{nt} [sic] Middleton to Superceede Smith, whose Commi∫sion was read to the Ships Company.

'Tuesday 20th January 1795. Ans^d the Sig^l for a Court Martial On Board the *St. George*. Washed the Lower Gun Deck.

Captain Smith, his first lieutenant and the master were all tried by court-martial. All three were found guilty of neglect and were dismissed the ship, the court finding that the proper precautions had not been taken to secure the masts.

The log shows that the Court Martial sat every day until 28th January, but then makes no further mention of it, indicating that it reached its verdict that day. The procedure was very long-winded because of the requirement that everything

---

[21] Captain of the frigate *Lowestoft* (more commonly referred to as '*Lowestoffe*') when Nelson entered her as a newly commissioned lieutenant. It is said that it was from him that Nelson had learned his aggressive attitude in battle.
This particular letter is wrongly dated January, 1794 (i.e. the previous year) in Nicholas 'The Dispatches of Lord Nelson', vol I, p347.

should be written down in longhand, first the questions and then the answers.[22] After it was over a new captain was appointed;

> 'Thursday 29th January 1795. Delivered to the *Agamemnon* 2 68 pound Carronades... Delivered to the *Cap^nt* and *Fortitude* One Pairs [sic] of Shrouds each & 2 – Do – to the *Prin. Royal.* Rec'd 4 Bullocks, at 10 AM Came on Board Cap^nt Littlejohn & his Commission Read to the Ship [sic] Company; opened 3 Casks of Pork...'

It would be interesting to know how these heavy 'smashers', weighing several tons each, were lifted off *Berwick's* fo'c's'le and onto *Agamemnon* without the help of *Berwick's* mast, yard and lifting gear; presumably, *Agamemnon* was close alongside and used her own lifting gear. Meanwhile, the men were not only concerned with repair work;

> '30th January 1795. Delivered 2 pairs of Main Shrouds to the *Britannia* & Shot Boxes, Wads &c. to the *Agamemnon*,' [followed by 40 68-pounder shot next day, and 103 more on 1st February.]

We should not under-estimate the difficulties *Berwick's* crew were facing. Her 'mainmast', the technical name for just the lower section of what we would call the main mast, weighed about 14 tons (excluding the 'fighting top') and was nearly ten ft in circumference. It was fabricated from long sections of timber, tightly bound and kept in place by iron rings at intervals, and 'stepped' onto the keelson. It was supported where it passed up through a substantial timber frame in the main deck, the 'partners', by heavy wedges. The 'topmast' fitted onto the top of the mainmast, the 'topgallant' to the topmast and the 'royal' (in light winds) to the top of that. The other two masts were made in the same way. In all, the masts, bowsprit and yards of *Bellerophon*, a somewhat similar '74', weighed more than 60 tons, her 'standing rigging' that supported the masts and bowsprit weighed 26 tons and her 'blocks' (pulleys) and the 'running rigging' that controlled the sails added another 27 tons.[23]

Jervis, a strong disciplinarian, later attempted to stop his married captains in the Channel Fleet from leaving blockade duty to rejoin their wives, on the pretext of having to return to port for repairs, by laying down strict maximum times for each type of repair. This gives a good idea of how long it took to step a new mast, as only a week was allowed for most repairs, but ten days were allowed for this task.

It is safe to assume that most of the sails, yards, running rigging and blocks had

---

22 'Life in Nelson's Navy', by Dudley Pope.
23 - ditto -

been removed before the disaster, but one doubts whether all three masts had, indeed, been totally stripped of every inch of standing rigging. The Court Martial would have heard detailed evidence on this, and that is probably why its proceedings took so long but, no matter how incompetent Captain Smith was, one cannot believe that he, his Master and his First Lieutenant had, in fact, left all three masts *totally* bare of *all* supporting rigging, as alleged. The ship's log must be correct on this, and not 'James', who probably worked on personal accounts many years later and certainly did not look at the log.

It is certain, however, from the log that the lower sections of all three masts and some of the topmasts as well went over the side and had to be recovered. A mainmast could not easily be replaced without the assistance of a 'sheer', an old hulk fitted with heavy lifting gear. This would lift up the mainmast and slot it back into position; the topmasts and spars could then be raised into position from on board. In the absence of dockyard stores and other facilities, all this would have taken a very long time.

During this period, when half *Berwick's* crew were still working on the shore trying to fabricate new masts and spars and generally clear up the mess, not only heavy guns and ammunition but also various petty officers were transferred to other ships. Unfortunately the rest of *Berwick's* log, like the muster book, is missing from then on, presumably weighted down in a canvas bag and thrown overboard before she later surrendered to the French.

After appointing Littlejohn to take over permanent command of *Berwick*, Hotham announced that he was sailing with the fleet for Leghorn, leaving *Berwick* there at Fiorenzo Bay on her own. His instructions to Littlejohn were simply to follow him to Leghorn as soon as he had rigged jury-masts. He made no arrangements whatsoever for her safety, not even leaving a sloop, let alone anything larger, for her protection. *Berwick* could have been taken, under tow, with the rest of the fleet, later that same day if necessary, but he was not prepared to wait.

Perhaps *Berwick's* condition was, in Hotham's opinion, worse than he earlier had been led to suppose. He probably decided she was hardly worth saving or, at least, that it was not worth putting the rest of his fleet at risk in order to protect her. She certainly had no chance of getting her main mast up again in a hurry – it must have been completely written off. It may be that Hotham had originally decided to wait because he was not prepared to leave such large amounts of salvageable spars, rigging and stores behind on shore, and now regretted it.

The log shows that Hotham ordered *Berwick* to give away her shrouds and parcelled out her best guns and men to other ships in his fleet. So he must have decided that was better to cut his losses and waste no more time at 'Feorenzo Bay', hoping that *Berwick* could find her own way back to Leghorn to rejoin the fleet when she was able to do so. To leave her unprotected was a distasteful decision for him to take, but how many ships would it have required to have afforded her adequate protection? Frigates, the obvious ships to assign to this task, were in desperately short supply. But, if *Berwick* was indeed badly damaged and in need of Leghorn's dockyard facilities, why on earth did Hotham decide to leave her behind, unprotected, at San Fierenzo Bay? Why not have her towed to Leghorn with the rest of the fleet to defend her?

As luck would have it, 15 French ships which were left behind unburned when Hood was kicked out of Toulon in December 1793 were preparing for sea. Their frigates had already been out to sea once, and had returned on 7 January with a long list of captures and 600 prisoners. When they learned that the British fleet had left Corsica and gone to Leghorn they hastily began to assemble a combined force to re-take Corsica. The fleet put to sea on 3 March with the 15 battle ships and six frigates. One of them was their new frigate *la Minerve*.

Meanwhile, Captain Littlejohn in *Berwick* had got three jury masts up and had completed his temporary repairs.[24] He was anxious to rejoin Hotham's fleet, but had been unable to get out of Fiorenzo Bay until 6 March because of contrary winds and a succession of north easterly gales.[25] These had already partially dismasted two of the French fleet which, unknown to him, were now approaching Corsica. Littlejohn set sail at 5 am the next day but at dawn the leading French frigate signalled back that she had seen *Berwick*, under jury masts, doing her best to sail out of the bay and follow the British fleet to Leghorn. The French fleet (flying Spanish colours to confuse Littlejohn) set all possible sail.

Berwick, still badly crippled but not taken in by the well-tried ruse of the enemy's false colours, was no match for them in terms of speed. She abandoned her course for Leghorn and ran, instead, for Bastia, on Corsica's east coast, where Littlejohn hoped for help. She was hotly pursued by the most leeward of the

---

[24] Nelson mentioned in a letter to his wife dated 25 February 1795 that *Berwick* had by then been repaired.

[25] A frigate could sail closer to the wind than a 'line-of-battle ship', and a modern yacht a great deal closer than either. By 'tacking' to and fro across the wind, a ship can gradually work her way to windward. But no sailing vessel can sail straight into the wind, or anything like it. This meant that a war ship could be stuck in port for days at a time, unable to leave because of contrary winds. Worse, she could be out at sea in a gale, near a safe harbour, but quite unable to get in to safety because the wind was against her.

French frigates, *Alceste* (36), closely followed by *la Minerve* and *Vestale*. By 11 am *Alceste* raised her proper French colours and opened fire on *Berwick's* lee bow within musket-shot range. *La Minerve* and *Vestale* positioned themselves on *Berwick's* quarter and, soon (according to the British, but denied by the French reports) two line-of-battle ships joined them.

Littlejohn hoped against hope that Hotham's fleet would by now be at sea again, and still kept sailing doggedly on for Bastia. But, luckily for Samuel and the rest of *Berwick's* crew, the French knew she was already 'in the bag'. They took good care not to hit anything other than *Berwick's* jury masts, rigging and sails. They did not want a smouldering hulk on their hands when, by exercising a little patience and restraint, they could take a '74' which, even though badly damaged by the falling masts, was still capable of a full repair and was otherwise in reasonably good condition.

Berwick, however, was determined to do all she could with her heavy 32-pounder guns to inflict as much damage as possible before the inevitable happened. By noon her rigging was cut to pieces and all her sails were shredded into ribbons, but she still managed, with one broadside, totally to disable one of the frigates, the *Alceste*, that had been rash enough to attack her.

It was at this point that a bar-shot, aimed at the rigging but fired too low, took the unfortunate Captain Littlejohn's head clean off, 'by which misfortune his Majesty has lost a most valuable and experienced Officer, who has left a widow and four small children', as Hotham later added in his Dispatch.

The bar-shot also severed the mainsail foot-rope which '....(it blowing strong) went all to pieces.' The first lieutenant Nisbet Palmer[26] assumed command and, seeing that further resistance was utterly useless against such enormous odds, hastily conferred with his brother officers and ordered *Berwick's* colours to be struck. All secret documents were hurriedly put into a weighted canvas bag and thrown over the side. It was all over by noon – the French report stated that the entire engagement had lasted only fifteen minutes.

On *Berwick*, because of the French wish to preserve her hull relatively unharmed, the captain's was the only death and only four of her seamen were wounded. Her officers and men were split up and divided between the French ships 'without being allowed to take any clothes except those on their backs' and, according to the reports at the time, were very badly treated by their captors. When the officers were released from captivity (which was not until 2 October

---

26 He later served on *Dreadnought* at Trafalgar.

1795 in their case) they were formally tried by court martial for the loss of their ship but honourably acquitted.

Leghorn was commonly used for "watering ship" and refitting, and it is likely that Hotham wanted the fleet to refit and repair their storm damage there, rather than at San Fiorenzo Bay where the facilities were only limited. Hotham had not, it seems, ordered his fleet away from San Fiorenzo Bay so suddenly on urgent Admiralty orders, on pressing diplomatic business, or for the prospect of battle with the French, glory and taking prizes. Nor was he, as Littlejohn had so urgently hoped, even at sea. On the contrary, he had sailed with his fleet majestically into Leghorn, where his officers spent long evenings at the opera whilst their seamen followed other pursuits which later landed many of them in the hospital at Ajaccio. Nelson even had time to sit for a miniature, which he sent as a present to his wife.

Hotham's official report, reprinted in the London Gazette, conveniently glosses over *Berwick*'s loss. No reason is given for his hasty departure from San Fiorenzo Bay. He certainly makes no mention of the need to escort a convoy, as suggested by Nelson in his chatty letter to Locker, so presumably it reached its destination unaided. No explanation is offered for leaving *Berwick* alone and totally unprotected. He simply says that he sent a cutter from Leghorn back to Corsica to order *Berwick* to join the fleet without further delay. She reported back two days later that the French were out again and that *Berwick* had been taken. This is confirmed by Nelson's 'Narrative' for 9 March 1795;

> 'At eight o'clock … signal for the *Tarleton* to proceed to St Fiorenzo, to order *Berwick* to join the Fleet.

> 'March 10th. At daylight, the *Tarleton* joined, and gave information that a boat came from off from Cape Corse, and told them that the *Berwick* had been taken on Saturday…'

Hotham straight away ordered his fleet to set sail from Leghorn with thirteen ships to seek out the French. Samuel's old ship *Diadem* was there in Admiral Sir Hyde Parker's division. The frigate *Meleager* (Captain Cockburn) was one of Hotham's 'repeaters'. The French were to windward off Corsica and sailing back towards Toulon when he found them. Nelson was leading the chase in *Agamemnon*. Although she was outdated and nearing the end of her useful life, she had recently had her bottom re-coppered and was the fastest 'ship of the line' in the fleet.

The French did not want to fight and were pressing on for Toulon. Many of their ships were lacking in officers as a result of the revolutionary purges, and only one third of their sailors had ever been to sea before. They were accompanied by *Berwick*, sailing in the middle of the fleet, protected by the other ships, with a French prize crew on board. Samuel and his shipmates were all locked down below, under an armed guard, on board other ships. No English prisoners were left on *Berwick*, whose prize crew naturally wanted no danger of them rising and re-taking their ship from their captors.

Agamemnon, some way ahead of the others, caught up with the 84-gun ship *Ça Ira* ('Large enough to take the *Agamemnon* in her hold', Nelson said) which had become detached from the others as a result of a collision. She had damaged her bowsprit and lost her main and fore topmasts. The frigate *Inconstant* attacked her, but had to retire, badly mauled. It is said, but without any great authority, that *Inconstant* may not have been the first there. Lieutenant Parsons, then a midshipman on *Victory*, recalls an amusing introduction to the battle;

> 'In that skirmish of Lord Hotham's, not particularly flattering to our naval prowess, [Lieutenant] Gibson, in the little *Fox*, ran under the stern of the *Ça Ira*, an eighty-gun ship, and loudly called on him to haul down his colours, or he would sink him. The Frenchman smiled with contempt, and the *Fox* broke all his stern windows with his six-pounders'.

After *Inconstant's* attack, *Ça Ira* was taken in tow by a frigate, and *Sans Culottes* (which, under the name *l'Orient*, blew up at Aboukir Bay) and *Jean Bart* stood by to protect her. Looking around him, Nelson saw that *Agamemnon* was alone, so he opened fire (unusually, for a British ship) at maximum range in the hope of doing some lucky damage, and lucky he was as nearly every shot hit home.

By skilful sailing he managed to stay dead astern of her (where he was safe from her deadly broadsides) until only 100 yards away. He would then suddenly turn at right-angles to her and deliver a broadside from close range, a 'raking shot', straight through the unprotected stern and stern windows of the enemy where she was most vulnerable, before executing another sharp turn that brought *Agamemnon* dead astern of her again. By doing this, his heavy guns double-loaded with both ball and 'canister',[27] he inflicted terrible injuries on her crew. His broadsides carried the full length of her gun decks, killing or wounding four hundred of them, even though the men would have been ordered by their officers to lie down for protection between their guns each time a broadside from astern was expected.

---

27 'Canister' consisted of a canvas bag (which broke up on being fired) containing standard 1oz. musket balls and was intended to kill and injure people. 'Grape shot' was similar, but the canvas bag was smaller and contained five or six larger iron balls, each about the size of a small apple, for damaging rigging, killing people or causing splinters of wood to fly off, injuring those nearby. Chain and bar shot were for damaging spars, sails and rigging.

The rest of the French fleet, seeing *Ça Ira's* predicament, turned round and headed back to render assistance. Hotham became worried at the possibility of losing *Agamemnon*. Nelson would have taken *Ça Ira* if Hotham had not signalled 'Return to Fleet' at the last moment. The French ship *Censeur* took *Ça Ira* in tow, and headed back towards Toulon. Next morning, however, *Ça Ira* and *Censeur* were both captured after a further tussle with the French and taken as prizes. Some of *Berwick's* men were found on *Ça Ira*, but not Samuel.

'James', not a noted Hotham fan, makes no mention of Nelson being recalled by Hotham and gives a somewhat different version of *Agamemnon's* part in this (giving *Inconstant*, Captain Freemantle, most of the credit for the damage to the already crippled *Ça Ira*);

> 'At about 9 a.m. this frigate [*Inconstant*] ranging up within musket shot on the larboard quarter of the French 80, gave her a broadside and stood on... The French frigate *Vestale* presently bore down, and, after firing several distant broadsides at the *Inconstant* as she ran by her, took the *Ça Ira* in tow. Having tacked, the *Inconstant* again passed under the lee of the two-decker, and fired into her. The latter, however, having ... cleared the wreck of her topmasts from her larboard side, opened a heavy fire from her lowerdeck guns... One of the shots, a 36-pounder, struck the frigate between wind and water, and compelled her to bear up.

> 'At 10h.45m A.M. the *Agamemnon* got upon the quarter of the *Ça Ira*, still in tow by the *Vestale*, and, aided for a short time by the *Captain*, continued a distant engagement with the crippled 80, until about 2h. 15m P.M.; when, several of the French ships bearing down to the protection of their disabled companion, the *Agamemnon* ceased firing, and dropped into her station in the line ... but the action terminated, for that day, when the *Agamemnon* had bore up.'

Hotham, pleased with himself that he had, for the moment at least, prevented the recapture of Corsica, refused to continue the chase. To Nelson's disgust, the rest of the French fleet got clean away. He was rowed across to Hotham's flagship to protest. Hotham merely replied; 'We must be contented, we have done very well.' Nelson, a prolific letter writer, then wrote to a friend;

> 'I believe [Hotham] heartily tires of his temporary command; nor do I think he is intended by nature for a Commander-in-Chief, which requires a man of more active turn of mind.'

His new friend Sir William Hamilton wrote;

> 'I can *entre nous* perceive that my old friend Hotham is not quite awake enough for such a command as that of the King's Fleet in the Mediterranean.'

Nelson, furious at the French fleet's escape, was even more annoyed when he learned, for the first time, that the escaping French fleet had included poor *Berwick* in their midst, and that Hotham had let them return safely to Toulon with *Berwick* their prize. Hotham spent the next three weeks in Leghorn or San Fiorenzo Bay, leaving Toulon completely uncovered, and Nelson's fury increased yet again when he heard that six more French ships from Brest had got into Toulon, safely and unopposed.

As naval prisoners of war were normally kept by the French at the nearest major naval port, it seems that the Blackmore family tradition that Samuel was held prisoner at Toulon is true. Neither side kept any proper records of prisoners. He would have been held in absolutely appalling conditions throughout the heat of the summer under what was called 'the Lion Sun'; conditions only equalled, if not exceeded, by the conditions in which the British kept captured French sailors.

On both sides, officers were usually allowed out on parole, but not common sailors, not the likes of Samuel! British sailors were normally kept in French prisons or old fortresses but, apart from the lucky few assigned to modern purpose-built prisons like Dartmoor, or the huge prisoner-of-war camp at Norman Cross by the A1 ('Great North Road' as some still prefer to call it) near Peterborough, most French sailors were kept by the British in old hulks. These were ships too old, rotten and water-logged to put to sea, but moored up in rivers and estuaries and crammed full with humanity, all battened down below under armed guard.

The worst example of British barbarism towards prisoners of war was perhaps the *Jersey*, an old 64-gun ship, stripped of her masts and rigging, that was moored off what is now Brooklyn Naval Yard on Long Island, New York, in the American War of Independence – what in the USA they refer to as 'the Revolutionary War'. Crammed with 1,000 prisoners at a time, 10,000 men are said to have perished in her and in her associated hospital ships (due not only to the diseases that were inevitable in such crowded conditions, but also to totally inhuman treatment and sheer brutality) in just three years from 1780 to 1783[28].

On 13 July Hotham was given a second chance – the opportunity of recovering his reputation – when the French fleet were again encountered off Hyères. *Meleager* was again acting as 'repeater'. But history tends to repeat itself. From eight miles astern of the van of his fleet, Hotham again became anxious and

---

[28] 'Recollections of the Jersey Prison Ship' by Albert Green, Applewood Books, Bedford MA, originally published in 1829.

ordered their return, even though they had by then attacked and set fire to the French *Alcide* which had blown up. Nelson explained his feelings of frustration to his old friend the Duke of Clarence in a letter of 15 July 1795;

'At noon the *Victory*, Admiral Man, with *Captain, Agamemnon, Cumberland, Defence,* and *Culloden,* got within gun-shot of the Enemy; when the wind failed us... At half-past three the *Agamemnon* and *Cumberland* were closing with an eighty-gun ship with a Flag, the *Berwick,* and *Heureux,* when Admiral Hotham thought it right to call us out of Action... Thus ended our second meeting with these gentry'.

So it had, after all, been possible to repair *Berwick* and restore her to the 'line'. But, this time, it was the French line.

Hotham's failure to press home the attack, in what became known as the 'Battle of Hyères', was a diplomatic disaster, as it convinced Britain's allies that they were on the losing side. It led, ultimately, to Austria's capitulation, an alliance between Spain and France, the loss of Corsica and the British abandoning the Mediterranean.

To the relief of all concerned, Admiral Sir John Jervis took over from Hotham that November. He had been delayed in taking command in the Mediterranean by parliamentary business, with what he saw as fatal results. He wrote to the First Lord;

'I have greatly to lament your Lordship did not dispatch me [sooner]. Hotham has a lot to answer for. What was done in his time was thanks to Nelson, who did wonders with the few ships Hotham would allow him.'

When Spain sided with France against Great Britain, relations between the Spanish and the English always remained cordial, and prisoners were treated reasonably. But this was not so with the French, although 'cartels' (exchanges of prisoners) were not all that uncommon at that stage in the war. Nelson wrote on 5 May to the father of a young officer taken prisoner;

'...three Cartels are expected from Toulon with [sick] prisoners; amongst whom I hope ... is your son.'

In all probability, Samuel spent the most uncomfortable time of his life in a hot, foeted prison cell throughout the whole of a long, hot Provençal summer in Toulon, totally despairing of ever seeing Devon and his family again. Food would have been minimal, and recreation non-existent. But hope springs eternal, and help was at hand. 'The Times' for 30 August 1795 reports;

'On 1st inst a flag of truce was sent to Toulon by Lord Hood,[29] proposing an exchange of prisoners [and it now seems certain that] an exchange of prisoners is....to take place.'

So how Samuel and his shipmates (including the marines) came to be returned is now also explained – although the officers and warrant-officers had to wait until 2 October before they were released. Samuel and the other men from *Berwick* were returned from Toulon (what ship they were transferred on is not recorded) and sent on board *Ça Ira* which was then serving as Guard Ship and base vessel (i.e. floating barracks) in San Fiorenzo Bay, Corsica. He is listed on her muster book with a large number of others as joining her 'from Cartel; late *Berwick*'. Samuel had already both seen action and enjoyed a period of French captivity whilst still only in his teens. He was shown in *Ça Ira's* muster book as 'supernumerary for victuals only'. In other words, to fit in with the naval accounting system, the ship's purser could claim for feeding him (at only two-thirds rations, as a passenger) but, as he was not part of her regular crew, he could draw no pay.

If Samuel had hoped to be given a few days shore leave to recover from his period in captivity, he was very much mistaken. The Navy was desperate for men – even more than before. On 21 September 1795 the London Gazette carried a Royal Proclamation extending the King's Bounty (recently doubled to £5 for every A.B. and £2.50 for every Ordinary Seaman volunteering to join the Navy) by providing £1 to any informer who should report where the Press Service could find a qualified A.B. or Ordinary Seaman hiding away. As Brian Lavery[30] points out, although exchanges of prisoners did take place from time to time, it was more difficult than in earlier wars because of the peculiar loathing that each nation now had for the other. Besides, the British had so many more French prisoners than they had British that it was sometimes difficult to arrange for an appropriate exchange. Samuel Blackmore's experiences of captivity and subsequent release must be the exception to the rule.

---

[29] This is difficult to understand, as Hood was involved in a disagreement with the Admiralty on 15 June 1795 over strengthening the Mediterranean Fleet, and had been recalled to London earlier that year. He was ordered to lower his flag and never went to sea again. Even though the final evacuation of Toulon had gone well, men were inevitably lost to the French, sailors as well as soldiers, in the earlier fighting. We must assume that this was a final piece of 'tidying up' which would have been left to Hood, as the Commander-in-Chief at the time, to sort out with his French opposite number some 18 months later.
[30] 'Nelson's Navy, The Ships, Men and Organisation 1793-1815' by Brian Lavery.

CHAPTER 3

In June 1795, the frigates *Dido* (28 guns, Captain Henry Towry, main armament only 9-pounders) and Nelson's old ship *Lowestoft* (32 guns) were sent to scout out Toulon and see what the French fleet there were up to. As it so happened, two French frigates, *la Minerve* and *Artémise* (36) had been sent out from Toulon on a similar mission.

They met north of Minorca at 8.30 am. *Minerve* commenced by trying to ram and board *Dido*, which put her helm hard over and was struck a glancing blow which entangled *Minerve's* bowsprit in her rigging. The attempt to board *Dido* was beaten off, but *la Minerve's* bowsprit snapped off and took with it *Dido's* mizzen mast. As they passed, side to side, more of *Dido's* rigging and some of her sails were torn off, but *Lowestoft* came up to assist and shot away *Minerve's* foremast, main and mizzen topmasts. *Artémise* fired two broadsides, one at *Dido* and one at *Lowestoft*, and then tried to escape, but *Lowestoft* went after her. On board both *Minerve* and *Dido*, frantic efforts were being made to clear away the damage so that they could recommence the contest. *Dido* recalled *Lowestoft*. She rejoined at 11.30 am and poured heavy fire into *Minerve's* quarter. *Dido* also managed to attack again, whereupon *Minerve* hailed to say that she surrendered and hauled down her colours.

It is interesting to compare the 'weight of metal', the broadside, that each ship could throw in this encounter;

Dido	156 pounds
Lowestoft	212 pounds
La Minerve	370 pounds
Artémise	283 pounds

Berwick's loss had thus been avenged. *La Minerve* may not have been a '74', a ship of the line, but the French had again lost a brand new frigate, heavily armed and of modern design, to an inferior force.

A report to the Admiralty, reproduced in the London Gazette, tells the story in the low-key, matter-of-fact terms that were customary;

'Evan Napean Eſq

'Dido Port Mahon June 27 1795

'I this day di∫pached the *Fox* Cutter to communicate to you that … we di∫covered and chaced [sic] Two French Frigates; after ∫ome manoeuvering they ∫tood towards us and … the *Dido*, leading down, commenced a clo∫e action with the headmo∫t of the enemy ∫hips which … was much di∫abled from the lo∫s of her bow∫prit, Forema∫t and Main-top-∫ail… The *Dido* having cleared the Wreck of the Mizen-ma∫t and bent on new Top∫ails, joined in ∫ecuring the Prize, *la Minerve*, a new Ship of 42 guns, Eighteen-pounders, on the Main Deck and 330 men, a remarkably fa∫t ∫ailer… Mr Douglas, the Boat∫wain, a de∫erving man, is killed… I propo∫e fitting Jury ma∫ts in the Prize, and proceeding to Ajaccio.

I remain with Re∫pect, Yours &c.

G.H.TOWRY.'

Three paintings in the National Maritime Museum's collection purport to show *Dido's* capture of *la Minerve*. The first shows two frigates passing, starboard to starboard, firing at each other at pistol-shot range, but the French ship has its bowsprit and jib-boom intact, which contradicts the above account. Another[31] shows two frigates in a duel, but there are lots of other ships around, which must also be wrong. A third, not painted until 1816, shows *la Minerve* in a very sorry state and is probably reasonably accurate. The best picture of the duel,[32] is in the members' bar of the 'In & Out', the Naval & Military Club. But by far the best way to find out what she was really like is to pay a visit to HMS *Trincomalee* at Hartlepool – a *Leda* class frigate launched in 1817, now fully restored and an amazing sight with her masts and fighting tops towering over the surrounding buildings. Although not to the same design as *Minerve*, she gives an accurate idea of the conditions in which sailors lived and fought on a frigate two centuries ago.

At Ajaccio (on the island of Corsica) *La Minerve* underwent a prolonged and extensive refit, after the pounding she had received from *Dido*. Samuel and the others on *Ça Ira* at San Fiorenzo were transferred to the frigate *Southampton* and, when she arrived at Ajaccio in August 1795, were drafted onto *la Minerve*.

When she joined the Royal Navy, Towry was given command of her; she was obviously considered a step up from the little *Dido*. Towry was later to command *Diadem* at the Battle of Cape St Vincent. According to *Minerve's* log book at the Public Record Office at Kew, he came on board on 7 August 1795 at Port Ajacia [sic] and read his commission to the officers and men who had been drafted

---

31 Reproduced in 'The Man who Burned the White House. Admiral Sir George Cockburn 1772-1853' by James Pack, 1987.
32 A print taken from Jenkins' Naval Achievements [1817] reproduced above.

onto her from her captor HMS *Dido*. Most of the 'crew', at that stage, were Corsicans – presumably the dockyard workers came under Navy discipline if they were working on a naval ship.

The process of refitting her proceeded agonisingly slowly. The log for 22 August records 'Rec'd on Board 50 fathms of Junk from the store ship'. This was old rope for picking to bits to make 'wads' for the guns, or even new ropes, as the Mediterranean Fleet were desperately short of most essentials, including rope. The crew were employed throughout August in spinning yarn – re-using old rope by picking it to pieces and then re-spinning it, first into single strands and then, by spinning single strands together to make cord, and then several cords to make a rope and so on until the desired diameter of rope had been made.

On 10 September, by which time 50 seamen had joined her from the *Southampton*, ex *Ça Ira* (including Samuel) they were busy setting up the 'standing rigging', the ropes that held the masts in place. Six weeks later, Samuel gave his old shipmates in *Diadem* a cheer, the log showing;

'Wednesday October 23rd. Arrived here 2 Ketches, Prizes to HM Ships *Diadem* and *Romulus*.'

On 28 October *Minerve* took on board 89 barrels of gunpowder. Many of the crew were falling sick so the captain ordered extra wine to be given to them. On 5 November they were fitting the 'running rigging' (the ropes that controlled the sails and raised and lowered the yards and spars). Towry was by now driving the crew as hard as he was able, as he was anxious to put to sea without any more delay. That day's log records;

'Punishd Richd. Cambridge with 2 dozen lashes for Insolence and Disobedience of Orders opened a cask of beef No 582 Cont 38 Double pieces.'

The log, solely concerned at this stage with recording stores taken on board and used, work done by 'the People' and routine matters, makes pretty dull reading. But Richard Cambridge was again given 3 dozen more lashes for 'mutinous Behavior' on 5 December, exactly a month since his earlier experience, and only the second of many more floggings for this unhappy man.

On Sunday 6 December Captain Towry had his ship's company mustered aft by divisions and read to them the Articles of War (mainly a litany of discipline and punishments). On 11 December the log records 'Departed this life Evan Owen issued extra wine to the sick 8½ gallons.' Next day it records 'Rec'd 4 puns and 2 Hds rum, sailed with HM Ships *Culloden* and *Diadem*, *Inconstant* & *Lowestoft*. Buried the deceased.'

From this point on the captain's log becomes even duller, recording endless days at sea with the rigging and sails being torn to shreds by gales, masts and spars broken, new topmasts being fitted and 'the People' being employed every day mending sails and rigging. On 2 April 1776 the log records;

'Moored Fiorenzo Bay [on the island of Corsica]. Came on Board Captain Charles Ogle and Superseded Captain H Towry at noon.'

And so the story continues; gales, repairs to the ship whilst at sea, men falling overboard, and endless bullocks being slaughtered for the crew's dinner. The only light relief recorded was 'Exercised the Great Guns' in July 1796.

La Minerve, launched in September 1794 and commissioned the following month, was one of several unfinished ships left 'on the stocks' which the allies had failed to destroy when they quit Toulon at the end of 1793. She was designed by J.M.B.Coulomb, one of France's two foremost frigate designers, and had been laid down in Toulon in 1791. She had an official complement of 11 officers and 335 men, and had a main armament of 28 French 'eighteens'. In addition she had twelve 8-pounders on her quarter-deck and two 36-pounder 'obusiers' (a form of French carronade) on her fo'c's'le.[33]

At 1,110 tons 'burthen' and 154'4" long at the lower deck she was bigger than most British frigates of that time. Samuel's first glimpse of her five months earlier (if, indeed, he had been able to see anything at all of Berwick's attackers through all the smoke of battle on her gun deck, which is highly improbable) had not been a happy one. But when he joined Minerve he realised that his luck had at last turned; she was of the most modern design, well built (even if not quite as solid and substantially built as a British frigate) and one of the best in the entire fleet.

At the risk of boring the reader, it may be convenient to pause here to consider la Minerve's manning levels and her armament when she joined the Royal Navy. First, her complement, how many men were actually on board? This is not easy to answer, as different figures are quoted. The French navy were not short of 'sailors' (although trained seamen were hard to come by) so French ships usually had more men than had the equivalent ships in the Royal Navy. This was because it was their policy to make use of their superior numbers by attempting to board whenever possible.

La Minerve was said to have had 330 men when in the French navy, as against her official complement of 346 officers and men. A figure of 286 men is given at the time when she joined the British Navy, but letters from her Purser to the

---

33 Cdr. Alain Demerliac, 'Nomenclature des navires français de 1792-1799' (Nice, 1979)

Captain two years later refer to a complement of 300 men, whereas her muster book plainly states an official complement of 250. Her Purser could neither have fed nor paid a single man beyond that number without an admiral's authority. In practice, at the best of times and even before allowing for death and injury, a ship would always be at least ten per cent. below her nominal manning level.

In those days a man did not 'join the Navy'. He signed on board a particular ship for the duration of her commission and, in theory, his obligation ceased when she was paid off. In practice, of course, a man on a homeward bound ship was usually taken off her and 'rolled over' into another outward bound ship. Even if he managed to set foot on dry land, the press service soon picked him up.

Jack Tar had no official uniform at that date. Officers had just adopted something like a common uniform according to rank, and some of the petty officers on a ship dressed in a similar fashion. The marines on every ship were, of course, resplendent in their scarlet uniforms and white pipe-clay belts and webbing. But the only 'uniform' for the common sailors was the checked shirts, short jackets and baggy trousers they all liked to wear. These were bought from the purser as 'slops' and the price deducted from their wages so, as all 'slops' were much the same, they had uniforms of a sort.

Everything in the Navy was 'rated'. Samuel was rated 'A.B.'. *La Minerve*, like other large frigates, was rated a 'fifth rate'. The number of officers, the number of men, the rate of pay of her petty officers, even the amount of iron ballast a ship was allocated, depended on her rating. With a fixed number of men per gun, eleven for a pair of 18-pounders, a ship's theoretical complement depended almost entirely on the size and number of guns she had – or, more precisely, the number of guns at which she was 'rated'.

It must be appreciated here that there is a world of difference between the number of guns at which a frigate was officially 'rated', and the total number of long guns, carronades and 'chasers' that she actually carried. When captured, *Minerve* had a total of 42 guns. Nelson said later that she had 44. The Victorian naval historian Clowes[34] happily quotes her as having 38, 40 or 42 guns, once even giving different figures on the same page. Many find this somewhat confusing.

The confusion is largely due to the introduction of 'carronades'. By that time, although the traditional 'long guns' of the Royal Navy continued to be the main armament of a ship, they were being supplemented, or even to some extent

---

[34] 'The Royal Navy. A History from the Earliest Times to the Present.' by W.L.Clowes, 1897 (reprinted 1996).

"GOVER'S New Improved Gun Carriage" a design for a new carriage for guns on the Carronade principle, from the Naval Chronicle (above and on opposite page)

replaced, by carronades. These were newly designed light-weight guns with short barrels but firing anything up to 24, 32 or even occasionally 64-pound balls. Most ships also had a couple of 'chasers' (smaller guns, probably 9-pounders with long barrels, but accurate at extreme range) mounted on the fo'c's'le facing forwards and probably two more at the stern. These, and the new carronades, were excluded from the gun count, which was solely concerned with a ship's primary and secondary armament.

What is certain is that *Minerve* was 'pierced' (i.e. had gun ports) for 30 guns on her upper deck.[35] The two forward-most of these were 'bridle ports', right up in the bows and facing forwards, and were for use only with long-range chase guns. The remaining 14 ports on each side were for her main armament, a total of 28 'eighteens' – 18-pounders – with lighter guns on her quarter-deck and fo'c's'le.

The French 'livre' was somewhat heavier than the English pound, so a French 18-pounder threw an iron ball of very nearly 20 pounds. Some books refer to *Minerve* as having 'long eighteens'. These were 9ft long and weighed over two tons each, exclusive of the weight of the carriage. They would have been normal on the upper gun deck of a larger ship[36] but in the Royal Navy they were, at that date, considered both too long and too heavy for a frigate, which would normally have the shorter and lighter 8ft gun. But the French thought differently and had built *Minerve* to carry them.

---

35 What the Americans call the gun deck – much less confusing.
36 The 32-pounder was, by now, the heaviest long gun normally found in the Navy, even on 'first raters', as experience showed that a bigger ball was too heavy for a man to handle reliably in battle.

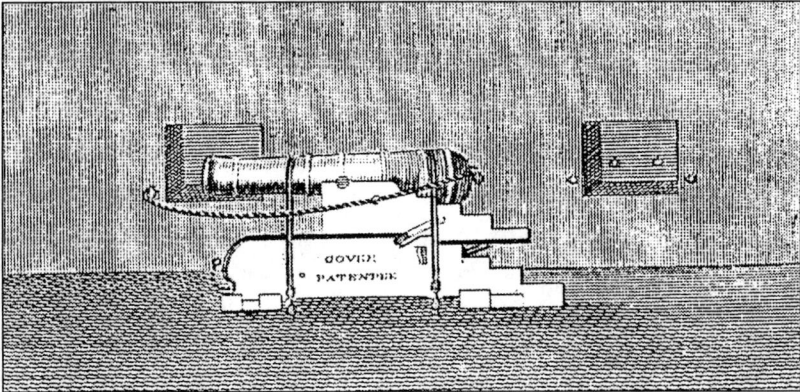

When *la Minerve* entered the British Navy, the French guns were taken out of her and replaced with standard British guns. This had to be done because it would have been impossible to keep stocks of non-standard French balls and cartridges, just for *Minerve* and a few other ex-French ships, at every supply depot on her station. She was then officially rated as a '36'. Because of the extra weight of iron shot they could throw, her 'secondary armament' (the 9-pounders on her quarter-deck and fo'c's'le) were replaced by eight 18-pounder carronades. The two 'obusiers' mounted on her fo'c's'le were replaced by two British-made 'smashers', 36-pounder carronades.

Some British captains thought that French frigates faced a heavy sea more happily if the forward pair of guns was removed, but there is no evidence that this happened to her in the British navy.

Minerve was re-rated as a '38' on her major refit in 1798. The Naval Chronicle, 1799, vol II contains a list headed 'The Present State of the Royal Navy', which

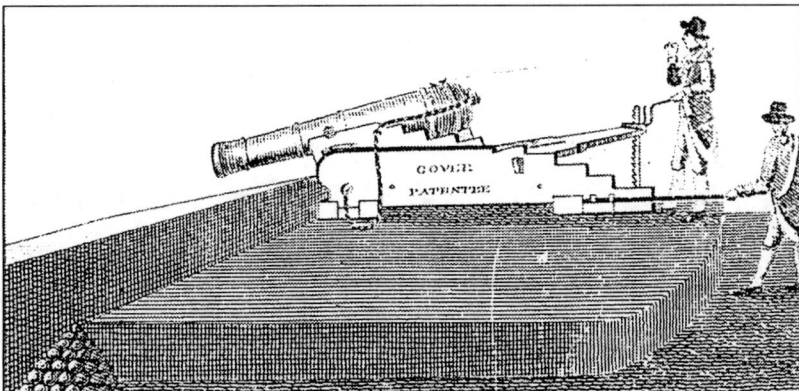

lists 'La Minerve, 44 guns, now at Portsmouth.' These would have been her 28 'long eighteens' plus 16 more guns – two bow chasers, two stern chasers, the two 'smashers' and two other carronades on her fo'c's'le and the eight carronades on her quarter-deck.

She was said by the French, when she was re-captured by them in 1803, to have had a total of 48 guns, her main armament of 'eighteens' plus fourteen 32-pounder carronades and six 'nines'[37] on her quarter-deck and fo'c's'le. If this was correct (and allowing for the confusion between 'nines' and 'eights') there must have been much experimentation in an attempt to find her ideal armament.

The final word on this can be left to 'The Sailing Navy List' by David Lyon, the standard reference work. This states that in the Royal Navy she had 28 18-pounders on her upper deck, eight 9-pounders on her quarter-deck plus two more on her fo'c's'le, six 18-pound carronades on her quarter-deck and two more on her fo'c's'le. No date is given. Perhaps at that stage she was still 'rated' as a '36' but, as Nelson said, carried 44 guns – except that this totals 46!

Carronades were much less accurate than the traditional long guns and could not be used at long range, that is beyond about four hundred yards. But this was no disadvantage in a Navy whose aim was to get as close as possible alongside the enemy[38] in order to pound them into pieces and kill their crews. Conversely the French captains preferred to aim high and attempt to dismast their British adversaries so that, using their superior numbers of men, they could board them. Experience showed that, in close combat, the 'weight of metal' fired in a broadside normally mattered most.

Being light, carronades were usually fitted on the quarter-deck and fo'c's'le. They were often loaded with 'canister' to clear the enemy's decks before sending across a boarding party. Firing 'canister' from close range, a carronade's effect on the officers and men exposed on the quarter-deck of the enemy ship opposite needs only to be imagined. Their mountings meant that they could be trained over a greater angle of fire than the old long guns, they only required a small gun-crew to handle them and a higher rate of fire could be achieved. Being lighter than a traditional long-barrelled gun, a ship with carronades could now carry a far

---

[37] Said by 'The Naval History of Great Britain' by William James, vol IV, to have been six 'long eights'.

[38] By tradition, the last signal flown from the admiral's flag ship as battle commenced was always 'Engage enemy more closely.'
Nelson's famous memorandum to his captains before Trafalgar said, '...in case signals can neither be seen nor perfectly understood, no captain can do very wrong if he places his ship alongside that of an enemy.' His friend and mentor, Capt. Wm Locker, had written to him from Lowestoffe in 1777; 'Always lay a Frenchman close, and you will beat him.'

greater weight of fire-power than before.[39] To start with, however, there were problems. For example, with some types of mounting, the new guns used to set fire to the rigging, and in *Minerve's* case the installation of carronades was allowed, but only on condition they were not fitted 'in the wake of the rigging',[40] i.e. not where the gun ports were situated between the shrouds.

Rate of fire was all-important, and the British seem to have had the advantage over the French and the Spaniards, but what rate could Jack Tar actually achieve? Oddly enough, the rate of fire possible in an 18th century ship is not known for certain. One shot a minute has been suggested; maybe this was possible for carronades or small guns on a frigate firing individually, as they normally did, but the rate of firing full broadsides on a three-decker may have been only one every three minutes. Collingwood (whose ship was first in action at Trafalgar) thought three broadsides in five minutes was about par (i.e. one every two and a half minutes) but had got that down to three rounds in three and a half minutes (i.e. less than two minutes per round) on *Dreadnought*, his previous ship. Dudley Pope [41] says that Collingwood managed three broadsides in ninety seconds (i.e. 45 seconds between each shot) and that, at Trafalgar, *Victory's* guns fired three rounds in two minutes – one minute between each – but where he got his information from he does not say.

Perhaps the best evidence of rates of fire comes from Napoleon, an expert artillery officer. He reckoned on only 20 shots per hour from his 24-pounder siege guns – i.e. one every three minutes – and this on dry land, but firing continuously over long periods. It is most unlikely that ships could have achieved a higher sustained rate of fire, but (as Collingwood seems to suggest) with fresh gun-crews perhaps the first few broadsides could have been fired off faster.[42]

Nelson insisted that all his crews should be trained to a high level of efficiency. Even if powder and cannon balls were too expensive to be used every day for gun drill, all the other aspects of gunnery were constantly practised against the lieutenant's stop-watch.

---

[39] 'Clowes' quotes numerous instances where French captains either had their guns' quoins (the wedges to raise or lower their elevation) planed down or even removed altogether, to force their crews to shoot high. Commenting on the speed of fire by carronades, he also quotes an example of a British ship fitted with carronades firing eleven broadsides to three by a French ship with traditional long guns.

[40] 'The Heavy Frigate' by Robert Gardiner, [Chatham Publishing, London, 1997] p27, quoting an Admiralty Order of June 1798.

[41] Pope, 'Life in Nelson's Navy'.

[42] For a detailed study of rates of fire and gunnery generally, see 'Frigates of the Napoleonic Wars', by Robert Gardiner, Chatham Publishing, London, 2000.

Shore leave was almost never allowed in English ports because of the risk of men 'running' – desertion. Cockburn, on one of his later ships, encountered an ingenious attempt at deserting. A man 'fell' overboard. His co-conspirators rushed to the jolly boat at the stern shouting 'man overboard', lowered it into the water and rowed as fast as they could to rescue him. Having done so, they just kept on rowing; the shore happened to be quite close.

Until the arrival of steam-power, which meant putting ashore for coal at frequent intervals, ships relied solely on wind-power and man-power. Misfortunes or battles apart, the ships in Nelson's time could and, when on blockade duty, did stay out at sea for months at a time. On one occasion Nelson did not touch dry land for two whole years and later, on blockade duty, his friend Cuthbert Collingwood did not even drop anchor for twenty-two months.

Collingwood's terrier Bounce was his only company, he said. Collingwood longed to see his family and home again. After Trafalgar, he was promoted Vice Admiral of the Red and made a baron. He wrote to his wife;

> 'I am out of all patience with Bounce. The consequential airs he gives himself since he became a right honourable dog are insufferable. He considers it beneath his dignity to play with commoners' dogs and truly thinks that he does them grace when he lifts his leg against them. This, I think, is carrying the insolence of rank to extreme.'

One day Bounce fell overboard and drowned. Within seven months his master died at sea (of what is believed to have been stomach cancer) without having seen his wife or home again.

A common sailor's only hope of setting foot on shore would often be to join a watering party in one of the ship's boats; ships needed to re-water every three months or so. But even that was back-breaking work as all the water was carried in barrels[43] which had to be man-handled back on board with no other help than a block and tackle.

That does not mean to say, however, that life in port was totally without diversions. Even if shore leave was not permitted, women were usually allowed to come on board when a ship was in port. Admiral Hawkins, whose account may be a little biased as he was known to be a religious bigot, wrote of the scenes on board when in harbour;

---

[43] In 1808, Lord Cochrane, then captain of *Impérieuse*, found himself off a hostile shore and desperate for water. Large bags were made from her studding sails, tightly stitched at the seams to make them nearly water-tight, and these were taken by boat up the Rhône until they reached fresh water. Towing the bags back to the ship and securing them alongside, the fire pumps quickly refilled all her water casks.

'It is well known, that immediately on the arrival of a ship of war in port, crowds of boats flock off with cargoes of prostitutes. Having no money to pay for their conveyance, the waterman takes as many as his boat will hold, upon speculation, and hovers round the ship until she is secured at her anchors and the necessary work done... The men then go into the boats and pick out each a woman (as one would choose cattle), paying a shilling or two to the boatman for her passage... Hundreds come off to a large ship. The whole of the shocking, disgraceful transactions of the lower deck it is impossible to describe – the dirt, filth, and stench; the disgusting conversation; the indecent, beastly conduct and horrible scenes; the blasphemy and swearing; the riots, quarrels and fighting which often take place, where hundreds of men and women are huddled together in one room as it were, in bed (each man being allowed only sixteen [sic] inches breadth for his hammock), they are squeezed between the next hammocks and must be witnesses of each other's actions; can only be imagined by those who have seen all this... giving way to every excess and debauchery that the grossest passions of human nature can lead them to.'[44]

Another account, along the same lines, is given by John Wetherell;[45]

'In the course of an hour the ship was surrounded with shore boats. First the Married men had liberty to take their wives on board then the young Men had their girls came off and took them on board, a curious sight to see boats crowded with blooming young girls all for sale. Our crew were mostly young men and caused the boatmen to have quick dispatch or as we usually term it a ready market; this business over, nothing particular occurred that day. Next morning it was found that there was two more women than men on board ... a mighty Jovial crew 616 souls on board. We took on Stores provisions and Water, and on the 4th orders were to send all the girls on shore except one woman to each mess and the married women certainly to have preference.'

Jack Nastyface[46] paints a vivid picture of the return of the bumboats (it is not hard to guess how they came by this name) when his ship the *Revenge* was due to put to sea;

'The word was now passed for the women to stand by and be ready to go on shore the next day. It is not the happiest moment of a sailor's life when he is due to be parted from his Nancy, but grieving's a folly and upon these occasions they generally throw grief and a temporary affection over the taffrail as

[44] Anon (Admiral Hawkins & others) Statement Respecting the Prevalence of Certain Immoral Practices in His Majesty's Navy, London, 1821
[45] 'The Adventures of John Wetherell', edited by C S Forester, Joseph, London, 1954.
[46] 'Nautical Economy, or Forecastle Recollections of the Last War', London, 1836.

commodities they do not take to sea with them. The boats being ready alongside, some of the men ... had brought bunches of onions ... and would very politely offer a few of the onions to those ladies who could not contrive to get up a cry at parting without their aid ... this creates a little merriment ... and is generally taken in good part by the ladies ... there were a few who felt the separation with concern; here and there one man would appear chap-fallen ... whilst others would shed a tear, as a dozen or two had plunged themselves into matrimony during the time we were in harbour...'

Officialdom turned a blind eye to the presence of women on board, even when the ship was at sea. An order to the Mediterranean Fleet from Admiral Jervis in 1796, with water conservation in mind, states;

'There being reasons to apprehend that a number of women have been clan-destinely brought from England to several ships....the respective Captains are required by the Admiral to admonish those ladies upon the waste of water, and other disorders committed by them, and to make known to all that on the first proof of water being obtained for washing from the scuttle-butt[47] ... in any ship, every woman in the fleet will be shipped home for England by the first convoy.'[48]

Later, he again had cause to order greater economy in the use of water by women, adding;

'It will become my indispensable duty to land all the women in the squadron at Gibraltar, unless this alarming evil is immediately corrected.'

There was nothing particularly unusual about women on board. Captain Freemantle had his wife with him on his ship at Nelson's disastrous attack on Santa Cruz in 1797. A painting of *Victory* at Trafalgar in the House of Lords clearly shows two women helping to serve the guns like anyone else.[49] Even on board *la Minerve* one of the petty officers had a wife with him.[50] In the army, five or six women were allowed to every company of 100 men or so; the non-commissioned officers drew lots to decide whose wives should accompany the regiment on campaign. Admiral Hawkins (quoted above) also wrote;

---

47 Barrel of drinking water kept at the foot of the main mast.
48 The Nelson Society's journal, the 'Nelson Dispatch', July 1996. Extracted from the *Naval Chronicle*.
49 After the battle, a cutter picked up a survivor from the *Achille* who turned out to be a woman. She had joined as a sailor, disguised as a man, to be with her husband. She was transferred to *Revenge* where, amongst all the other French sailors who had already been rescued and were now being held prisoner, she found her husband.
50 R.Morriss, 'Cockburn and the British Navy in Transition. Admiral Sir George Cockburn, 1772-1853.' Exeter University (1997).

'In 1808, Captain —— even allowed nine women to go to sea in the ship... Of one, I recollect it being stated that she admitted nineteen men to her embraces in one night.'

The expression 'son of a gun' thus probably meant just that; with fifteen men to a standard naval 32-pounder gun-crew, anyone sired on board a 'ship-of-the-line' could never be sure of his paternity. Captain Gascock wrote in 1836;

'This day the surgeon informed me that a woman on board had been labouring in child for twelve hours, and if I could see my way to permit the firing of a broadside to leeward, nature would be assisted by the shock. I complied with the request, and she was delivered of a fine male child.'

Turning to the men, it usually took several years to gain promotion from Ordinary to Able Seaman. Much depended on the 'rating' given to a man by the first lieutenant on joining ship – a cause of great dissatisfaction in the Navy. An Ordinary Seaman was expected to be able to 'hand, reef and steer', to man the yard-arms, handle the sails, tie knots, know all the different ropes and generally be competent at all the day-to-day things that needed doing on board ship, as well as man his gun. But an A.B. had also to be able to take soundings with the lead line at night, sew and mend sails and take the wheel, and do all these things reliably under adverse conditions.

Like *la Minerve*, a third of all British frigates had been captured from the French. They were generally a little larger than those of British design, which were usually rated as being of 28-36 guns. Having somewhat finer lines, they were nearly always a little faster, too. But that does not necessarily mean that they were better ships. British frigates were not designed for ultimate speed, but as much for their qualities in a gale and a heavy sea. They usually had more substantial 'scantlings' and fastenings too – their heavier hulls required less ballasting. Not everyone agreed that French designs were automatically better than the British. It was soon realised that, though many were slightly faster under ideal conditions (mainly because longer ships sail faster than shorter ones) frigates of British design were often superior in terms of seaworthiness and survival when it came to blockade duty in Atlantic winter gales. Gabriel Snodgrass, of the East India Company and their equivalent of Surveyor to the Navy, published an open letter to Dundas, Treasurer to the Navy, in 1797;

'In my opinion, a great deal too much has been said in favour of French ships. I cannot see any thing worthy of being copied from them but their magnitude; they are, in other respects, inferior to British ships of war, being slighter and weaker....and they likewise commonly exceed the old ships of the present Navy in the absurd tumble-home of their topsides....'

A British-built frigate was said to be able to sail at a maximum of around 12½ to 13 knots (15 mph) with her bottom cleaned; Dudley Pope[51] quotes an example of a British frigate averaging 14 knots for eight days in trade winds with nearly all possible canvas set. Being a bit longer and having finer lines, *la Minerve* could probably just top that under ideal conditions. It has been pointed out,[52] however, that ships' speeds were over-stated for two reasons; the standard Admiralty half-minute glass in fact measured only 28 seconds, not 30, and the standard spacing of the knots on the log line at one fathom intervals gave an even greater distortion. The result was that a ship's stated speed of 13 knots would in fact be no more than 11½ knots (about 13 mph) by modern reckoning.

To be on a frigate was what every would-be sailor dreamed of. To have served on board a famous 'first rate' ship of the line may have been something to tell your grandchildren about but, rather like destroyers in the 1939-45 war, frigates had all the glamour. It was often financially rewarding to serve on a frigate too, even for men on the lower deck; being fast, and usually operating on their own, the opportunities to earn prize money (and 'head money') by capturing enemy shipping (and men) were far greater than in a big ship. Ships of the line – i.e. battle ships and cruisers that could both deliver and withstand withering broadsides – usually operated in groups – 'the Line'. But frigates were kept out of 'the line' because to pit them against battle ships would have been suicide – they were only lightly built and lightly armed. They only cost half as much to build as a 'seventy-four'.

Frigates were mainly built for speed. British frigates were usually somewhat more sturdily built than their French counterparts, and had to be able to carry provisions for six months – a consideration which did not apply to French frigates which were, therefore, usually slightly lighter. Their purpose was to be 'the eyes of the fleet', very fast and capable of sailing slightly closer to the wind than a battleship. With a frigate over the horizon on each side, their mast-tops just visible, a 'ship of the line' searching for the French could, in theory, sweep a swathe 50 miles wide, or nearly 100 miles if there were four frigates.[53] Nelson never had enough of them, and swore in 1798 that 'Was I to die at this moment, Want of Frigates would be found stamped on my heart.'

---

51 Pope, 'Life in Nelson's Navy'
52 Gardiner, 'Frigates of the Napoleonic Wars'.
53 In practice, a frigate's flag signals (they were large, usually 12ft x 10ft) could not be read at more than six or seven miles. If she was to leeward of the fleet, it would also take a long time to beat up to windward to a point where she could send flag signals. Thus a 'sweep' would in practice usually be much narrower than this. Alternative signals were sometimes agreed, e.g. letting topsails fly for 'enemy in sight', so a reasonably wide sweep could still be possible under ideal circumstances.

An officer stood a greater chance of attracting official notice, and therefore of gaining promotion, on a 'line-of-battle' ship. But a common seaman infinitely preferred the easier life, the camaraderie and the more intimate atmosphere on board a smaller ship – the smaller the better. Besides, frigates and other small ships usually operated close inshore. Here the chances of capturing enemy coastal shipping – and, hence, of gaining some 'pewter', as they called prize money – were correspondingly greater.

Discipline on an East Indiaman was lighter than in a King's Ship and, after his experience in the cutters *Brazen* and *Kite*, Samuel Blackmore would have found life on a frigate a little more formal and intimidating, but infinitely preferable to life on a '64' or '74' like his old ships *Diadem* and *Berwick*. It was more rewarding, too; as we shall see, the gathering of 'pewter' featured large for those on *la Minerve*.

Living conditions on a 'ship of the line' were cramped beyond belief. On *Victory*, with three gun decks, the crew of 800 or so seamen and marines all hung their hammocks on the two lower gun decks, and ate there in messes of eight or so at tables slung between the guns. The head-room on the gun deck was about five feet; experience showed that any less meant it was too cramped for the efficient handling of the 'great guns' whereas, on the orlop and other decks not housing guns, less than five feet of headroom was normal. Each man was allowed 14 inches for his hammock but, as they operated in two watches with one always on duty – except when in port – a man effectively had 28 inches of space.

From the sailors' point of view, a major advantage of being on a frigate, rather than a 'ship of the line', was that the lower deck (the 'berth deck' in America) was entirely free of guns and there was therefore much more living room. There was even enough space for most men to have their own sea chests on board – not possible in a larger ship.

With the lower gun ports only a short distance above the water-line, the huge guns on the lower deck of a large ship (usually 32-pounders) could often not be used in rough weather or when she was heeled over, beating against the wind. But in a frigate, there was only one gun deck – the 'upper deck' (the 'gun deck' to the Americans). There was therefore normally more 'freeboard' between the water level and the gun ports, so she could fire her guns when heeled over. However, some frigates (particularly those of French design) were inclined to heel right over in a blow, with the water almost level with the gun ports. Firing to leeward then became difficult, if not actually impossible.

Aiming a gun was not easy. Proper gun sights (useless unless the gun captain could see anything through the gun-smoke, which was unlikely) were not introduced until some years later. He had to judge the gun's elevation by aligning two notches on the sides of the gun barrel, then judge the aim by looking along two notches on the top – and do this through the fog of gunsmoke from the previous broadside that filled the gun deck and billowed out of his gun port. He also had to allow for the roll of the ship and the slight but measurable delay in the actual firing of his gun;

> 'It was always necessary that he who points the gun should have judgment of the ship's motion, to do execution; for if the side be rising, he must take his aim below the water's edge, or he'll fire over the object; if it be lowering, he must level above the gun-wale, or he will fire into the water.'[54]

It was not until the 1812 war, prompted by the lethal accuracy of American gunnery, that any attempt was made to arrange for properly aimed broadsides. Captain Broke, on the frigate *Shannon*, provided sights and plumb-bobs at his own expense, and had quadrants marked out on the deck round each gun. This was so that all guns on that side could be given the same elevation and trained onto the same bearing. The captain on his quarter-deck, by monitoring the enemy's bearing, could then order all the guns to be fired at the moment she reached the bearing to which they had been aimed, gun-smoke not withstanding.

What was hard labour at the best of times in a big ship – hauling the guns back to reload, and running them out again ready to fire – became very hard work indeed for a depleted, battle-weary and exhausted gun-crew on a frigate's steeply slanting gun deck. It was not quite so bad when firing to leeward (so long as the sea was not slopping in through the open ports) as the recoil of a heavy cannon would send it back 'uphill' at least part of the way, and running it out again was gravity-assisted. But firing to windward was the problem. Running a two-ton gun back to reload was, of course, accomplished easily enough thanks to the combination of gravity and the gun's recoil, but running it out again, hauling that weight up a steeply sloping deck, was not for the weary or faint-hearted. It was also difficult to elevate a gun high enough (firing to leeward) or to depress it sufficiently (when firing to windward) if the ship was heeling right over.

Food was, however, the same throughout the Navy – it was, of course, different for officers but, for the 'People' as the officers referred to their crew, quite disgusting by modern standards! For sailors on the lower deck, food largely

---

54 'The Narrative of William Spavens', with introduction by N A M Rodger, Chatham Publishing, 1998

consisted of 'bread' – i.e. ships biscuit, which was full of weevils – salt pork or beef (except in port, when fresh meat was usually available) and mushy peas. The beef was so hard that you could use it for carving; it took quite a good polish! They were also allowed a gallon of beer a day[55], or the equivalent in wine when in the Mediterranean, or their traditional 'grog' served daily at the foot of the main mast – a half of a pint of strong rum per man, mixed with three parts of water.

Bernard Coleridge, an 11-year-old midshipman at the time when Nelson was also a 'snotty', wrote home from the blockade off Brest;

> 'We live on beef which has been ten or eleven years in corn and on biscuit which quite makes your throat cold eating it, owing to the maggots which are very cold when you eat them, like calves' foot jelly or blomange, being very fat indeed. Indeed I do like this life very much... We drink water of the colour of the bark of a pear-tree with plenty of little maggots and weevils in it and wine which is exactly like bullock's blood and sawdust mixed together. I hope I shall not learn to swear...'

Nelson is said to have sworn frequently. According to one of the books by Patrick O'Brian, an expert on the language of the period, most things were called 'the fucking sod', so one doubts if Midshipman Coleridge would have refrained from swearing for long. He was killed falling from the rigging three years later.

Also the same throughout the Navy in Samuel's day, but later abolished, was the Bosun's 'start' – either a two foot length of rope or a short cane with which he 'started' (i.e. encouraged) slow movers.

Everything centred on the guns. These were arranged in pairs, one on each side of the ship, with about 6ft 6ins between each gun. Fighting ships, whether frigates or 'ships of the line', were little more than floating gun platforms; there were no concessions to luxury. On *Victory*, even the Admiral had to share his tiny sleeping cabin with a 12-pounder. A pair of 18-pounders had, when the ship was fully manned, a crew of eleven men shared between the two guns, five to each and a 'gun captain' over both of them. It was not often that both sides of the ship (especially on a frigate) were firing at once, so the two halves of the crew were largely interchangeable. A man's normal 'action station' would be at his gun. But each man would also have another position, such as 'topman', manning the pumps, fire duty or boarding party, so when in action the gun-crew could, in practice, be severely depleted.

---

55 i.e. 8 pints. Anyone drinking more (by illegally buying someone else's beer ration) was 'one over the eight'.

That Samuel was a 'topman' – having to go up the mast to tend the sails in all weathers – is probable for two reasons. First, he had been a sailor from a young age, and must (as an A.B.) already have been experienced 'up aloft'. Generally, it would take too long to train 'landsmen' (such as those brought in by the press-gangs who were not already seamen, 'Lord Mayor's men', debtors and convicts released from prison) to work at 100 feet or more above the deck, up a swaying mast in a gale, so they usually landed the deck-based jobs. The sail-handling teams were, correspondingly, made up mainly of proper seamen who could stand, barefoot, on a foot rope stretched below a spar in a winter's howling gale, their elbows locked over the ice-covered spar whilst they dealt with the sails. Secondly, prize crews were all picked men and, of necessity, those who could reliably handle the sails on a strange ship – and Samuel was, as we shall see, picked to join the prize crew put on board *Sabina*.

If a sailor's life was tough, for others not in the Navy (farm labourers, for example) life was often a great deal tougher. By today's standards, discipline on board ship was often harsh and justice rough, but so they were on dry land. A sailor was more or less guaranteed three square meals[56] a day, a large quantity of alcohol, and a comfortable hammock to sleep in. But Wellington's soldiers in the Peninsular War had none of these advantages. They often slept out in mid-winter with their hair, tied in a pigtail as Samuel's was, stuck to the ground next morning with frost. They marched for days on end through deep snow without food and with their comrades dying all round them.

"Interieure de la batterie d'une Frigate", c.1820

---

56 Sailors ate off square wooden platters – which is why we still call it a 'square meal'. The raised rim was called the fiddle, so anyone having his platter over-full had obviously been 'on the fiddle'.

CHAPTER 4

On 19 August 1796, *la Minerve's* new captain came on board. He immediately had all hands mustered aft at the capstan-head and read aloud his commission to them – his personal orders to assume command. He was George Cockburn, then aged 24, with a second epaulette only recently added on his shoulder to show that he was now a 'post-captain' of three years standing.[57]

Cockburn was only eight when he officially started his naval career. He was nominally entered on a ship's books as a 'captain's servant', but was in fact sent to a nautical training college and did not actually join a ship until he was 14 – quite old in comparison with others, it being a common view amongst senior officers that, unless a boy was at sea by the age of 11, he would never make a good officer.

He was helped by being Nelson's protégé. He had been appointed the tenth and junior lieutenant on Admiral Hood's flagship *Victory* at a time when the Navy was rapidly expanding. Those senior to him were soon promoted so, within a matter of months he found himself First Lieutenant and in October 1793 was given command of the sloop *Speedy*, 14 guns. That autumn, Admiral Hood had set up a small squadron under Captain Sutherland on *Diadem* (on which Samuel was then serving) to prevent the so-called neutral Genoese from supplying corn to the south of France. In a severe storm, *Diadem* withdrew to the calmer water of Hyères bay, near Toulon, to repair her storm damage. One by one the other ships also had to withdraw with storm damage but Sutherland was astonished, on returning in *Diadem* to Genoa after the storm, to find that little *Speedy* had alone remained on station throughout.

The impossible had been accomplished – but by a tiny vessel, not a 'ship of the line' – and the blockade had thus been maintained. Sutherland wrote a most appreciative letter about Cockburn to Lord Hood. The letter, sealed of course, was entrusted to Lieutenant Cockburn to take to his admiral on *Victory* and, on reading it's contents, Hood decided to give him his captaincy as soon as a vacancy cropped up. Cockburn was therefore given command of the frigate

---

57 It must have looked a bit odd, but post-captains of under three years seniority only had one epaulette. The Captain's Commission was a fearsomely worded document, ending with '...you will answer to the contrary at your peril'.

Meleager, 36 guns, in February 1794 (after a brief appointment as acting captain of the frigate *Inconstant*) and made a 'post captain' at the age of only 21.[58] Good though she was, Nelson wrote to Hood asking him to give Cockburn a better ship, and this Hood did as soon as he could. Hood said that Admiral Hotham's nephew had the prior claim, based on seniority, but thought it unlikely that Hotham would want command of *la Minerve*. Just as well, as we shall shortly see.

On gaining command of *la Minerve* in 1796, Cockburn took with him his First Lieutenant, Jonathan Culverhouse, who seems to have been a popular man when he was Flag Lieutenant on the *Edgar*. He;

> 'would use a single-stick, with which he was superior to anyone in the fleet. He was a very clever fellow, full of fun and drollery, and sung humerous songs in the most comic style.' [59]

Cockburn also took with him his 'Third', Thomas Masterman Hardy (later Nelson's friend and *Victory's* captain at Trafalgar) who entered *Minerve* as her Second Lieutenant, together with five mature midshipmen with an average age of over 30. 26 seamen also came with him from *Meleager*, and were swapped for 18 of *Minerve's* men – no doubt the more unsatisfactory members of her crew! Culverhouse had first come to Nelson's attention when, as Lieutenant in charge of *Meleager's* boats, he had participated in a 'boat action' at Loano in April 1796. Boats from *Agamemnon* and three other ships 'cut out' four transports under the cover of shore batteries, but *Agamemnon* was the only vessel to be hit.[60]

The log shows that *la Minerve's* new commander found her not to be in good condition;

'IN BARCELONA ROADS

> 'Monday August 22nd 1796 ... carpenter employed repairing Quarter-deck (where it was rotten)...

> 'Wednesday August 24th 1796... People employed ... junk'd up a part of the Best Bower Cable finding it rotten...

> 'Thursday August 25th 1796... Carpenters at work upon the Quarter Deck and Cabin berth Head...'

Nelson briefly transferred his Commodore's broad pendant from *Captain* to *Diadem* at Corsica that autumn. *Minerve's* first task under Cockburn was to

---

58 Nelson became post-captain at the age of 20.
59 Gardner, 'Above and Under Hatches'.
60 Letter from Nelson to Jervis, 25 April 1796
61 Now called Livorno.

assist Nelson in stopping ships entering or leaving Leghorn[61], now held by the French. On 9 September a ship left harbour and attempted to escape, but she was driven ashore after hoisting French colours. *Minerve's* boats managed to tow her off again and took her as a prize, her first under her new captain. Next, she assisted in taking a small island off the Italian coast, Capria, landing troops, stores and guns there, and fetching water for the troops, together with large quantities of wine and brandy for them. Cockburn was said to have distinguished himself, and *Minerve's* crew were probably involved in the fighting. In October, *Minerve* went back to the blockade of Leghorn.

Napoleon had over-run most of Italy. The war was going very badly indeed, and all Great Britain's friends except Portugal deserted her. Genoa and Leghorn were now closed to them, the Spanish had declared war on Great Britain and their fleet of 26 ships of the line was somewhere (nobody knew where) in the Mediterranean. Corsica was about to be abandoned. Elba was the only safe refuge east of Gibraltar. Supplies were desperately short. Nelson wrote to Cockburn;

> 'I have orders from the Admiral viz. you are to put the captain, officers and men to ⅔ allowance[62] of all species of provisions, except wine and spirits, and you are to direct them to take especial care that the officers of any distinction, are not allowed a greater proportion than the men.'

Blockade duties continued until the middle of November, by which time the evacuation of Corsica had been completed. *Minerve* returned to Gibraltar on 9 December 1796, when a gale caused many vessels, *Minerve* included, to drag their anchors. One ship was lost, and several more were damaged; *Minerve* lost a large quantity of anchor cable and an anchor.

Next day Nelson (then a commodore with *Captain*, 74 guns, as his flag ship) was ordered to cover the evacuation of the island of Elba and withdraw the soldiers and the military and naval supplies there. *Captain* could not be spared so he was assigned *Minerve* and another frigate, *Blanche* (Captain Preston) for this purpose. Transferring his commodore's 'broad pendant'[63] from *Captain*, he hoisted it on Cockburn's *Minerve* as his flag ship. Samuel Blackmore, as an A.B. on *Minerve* at that time, could thus indeed truthfully say that he had served directly under the great man himself.

---

62 The men could claim compensation for short measure.
63 Admirals flew their own large red, white or blue ensigns (somewhat squarer in shape than today's rectangular flags) from the masthead. Commodores had a large 'swallowtail' pennant, nearly always called a 'pendant'. A ship with only her own commander on board flew a long streamer, sometimes as long as 24 yards.

Minerve had only just left Gibraltar and was off Cartagena on 19 December 1796 when two Spanish frigates, the *Santa Sabina* (40 guns) and the *Ceres*, gave chase. It was night time. Nelson hailed and called on *Sabina* to surrender. The reply came, in perfect English, 'This is a Spanish frigate, and you may begin as soon as you please.' *Minerve* took on *Sabina*, but only after three hours 'hard pounding', during which she lost all three masts, did her captain agree to surrender. *Minerve* lost 7 killed and 44 wounded. Three hours action must have been totally exhausting for the gun-crews, although in this action (as *Minerve* only had one adversary) both sides of the gun deck would not have been firing at the same time. However, the ship was constantly being manoeuvred as the two combatants sought the advantage, so members of gun-crews whose other duties included sail handling were frequently called from their guns to man the braces and trim the sails to the best advantage.

"Engagement between Minerve *and* Sabina*" from Southey's Life of Nelson.*

The Captain's log (the Master's log is similar but even briefer) outlines the engagement, without either heroics or Nelson's references to his own part;

> 'At 5 spoke HM *Blanche* and ordered her to stand 20 miles NE by E; brought onto the Starbd tack. At 10 the *Blanch* [sic] made Sigl to speak to us, bore down on hr, the captain told me he saw 2 Spanish Frigates to Leeward, Clear for Action & bore down, at 20 minutes before 11 I passed under the stern of one of theirs which I hailed, knowing it to be a Spaniard & not being answered I commenced Action with her by firing a broad side into her, at 11 saw *Blanche* engage the other... At 12 past 11 saw the Mizzen

Mast of the Frigate I was engaged with fall, wore ship occasionally to prevent her getting to Leeward which I saw she endeavoured to effect. At 20 past one she hailed us & struck her Colours, I sent the 1st Lieut to take Poſſeſsion of her, he sent the Spanish Capt. on board who surrendered himself & gave up his sword to me. His name was Don Jacobo Stewart ... took her in tow & made sail to ye SE.'

Nelson, never slow to dramatise an already dramatic episode, wrote;

'I have no idea of a closer or sharper battle: the force to a gun the same, and nearly the same number of men; we have two hundred and fifty. I asked him several times to surrender during the action, but his answer was "No Sir, not whilst I have the means of fighting left." When only he himself of all the other Officers was left alive, he hailed, and said he could fight no more, and begged I would stop firing.'

When the Spanish captain came on board *Minerve* and surrendered his sword, the reason for his perfect English was discovered; he was Don Jacobo Stuart, the great grandson of King James II of England, by Arabella Churchill, the king's mistress. Nelson returned his sword as a mark of respect for his gallant fight.

Perhaps the most gripping account of a frigate in action, a British frigate being pulverised by an American frigate superior to her in every way, is that given by a powder-monkey on the *Macedonian* in action against the *United States* in the war of 1812.[64]

'We had scarcely finished breakfast, before the man at the mast-head shouted, 'Sail-ho!'

The captain rushed upon deck, exclaiming, 'mast-head there!'

'Sir!'

'Where away is the sail?'

The precise answer to this question I do not recollect, but the captain proceeded to ask, 'What does she look like?'

'A square-rigged vessel, sir,' was the reply of the look-out.

After a few minutes, the captain shouted again, 'Mast-head there!'

'Sir!'

'What does she look like?'

'A large ship, sir, standing towards us!"

---

[64] 'A Voice from the Main Deck' by Samuel Leach, re-published by Chatham Publishing, London, 1999.

'By this time, most of the crew were on deck, eagerly straining their eyes to obtain a glimpse of the approaching ship and murmuring their opinions to each other on her probable character. Then came the voice of the captain, shouting, 'Keep your silence, fore and aft!' Silence being secured, he hailed the look-out, who, to his question of 'What does she look like?' replied, 'A large frigate, bearing down upon us, sir!'

'A whisper ran along the crew that the stranger ship was a Yankee frigate. The thought was confirmed by the command of 'All hands clear the ship for action, ahoy!' The drum and fife beat to quarters; bulk-heads were knocked away; the guns were released from their confinement; the whole dread paraphernalia of battle was produced; and after the lapse of a few minutes of hurry and confusion, every man and boy was at his post, ready to do his best service for his country... A few of the junior midshipmen were stationed below, on the berth deck, with orders, given in our hearing, to shoot any man who attempted to run from his quarters.

...We had been told ... that frigates in the American service carried more and heavier metal than ours. This, together with our consciousness of superiority over the French at sea, led us to a preference for a French antagonist.

As the approaching ship showed American colors, all doubt of her character was at an end. 'We must fight her,' was the conviction of every breast... The guns were shotted; the matches lighted; for, although our guns were all furnished with first-rate locks they were also provided with matches, attached by lanyards, in case the lock should miss fire...

My position was at the fifth gun on the main deck. It was my duty to supply my gun with powder, a boy being appointed to each gun in the ship on the side we engaged, for this purpose. A woollen screen was placed before the entrance to the magazine, with a hole in it, through which the cartridges were passed to the boys; we received them there, and covering them with our jackets, hurried to our respective guns. These precautions are observed to prevent the powder taking fire before it reaches the guns.

Thus we all stood, awaiting orders, in motionless suspense. At last we fired three guns from the larboard side of the main deck; this was followed by the command, 'Cease firing; you are throwing away your shot!'

Then came the order to 'wear ship,' and prepare to attack the enemy with our starboard guns. Soon after this I heard a firing from some other quarter, which I at first supposed to be a discharge from our quarter deck guns; though it proved to be the roar of the enemy's cannon. A strange noise, such as I had never heard before, next arrested my attention; it sounded like the tearing of sails, just over our heads. This I soon ascertained to be the wind of the enemy's shot.

The firing ... recommenced. The roaring of cannon could now be heard from all parts of our trembling ship, and, mingling as it did with that of our foes, it made a most hideous noise. By-and-by I heard the shot strike the sides of our ship; the whole scene grew indescribably confused and horrible; it was like some awfully tremendous thunder-storm ... only, in our case, the scene was rendered more horrible than that, by the presence of torrents of blood which dyed our decks.

...I was busily supplying my gun with powder, when I saw blood suddenly fly from the arm of a man stationed at our gun. I saw nothing strike him; the effect alone was visible; in an instant the third lieutenant tied his hand-kerchief round the wounded arm, and sent the groaning wretch below to the surgeon ... the boys belonging to the guns next to mine were wounded in the early part of the action, and I had to spring with all my might to keep three or four guns supplied with cartridges ... a man, who saw one of them killed, afterwards told me that his powder caught fire and burnt the flesh almost off his face. In this pitiable situation, the agonized boy lifted up both hands, as if imploring relief, when a passing shot instantly cut him in two.

I was an eye-witness to a sight equally revolting. A man named Aldrich had his hands cut off by a shot, and almost at the same moment he received another shot, which tore open his bowels in a terrible manner. As he fell, two or three men caught him in their arms, and, as he could not live, threw him overboard. The battle went on. Our men kept cheering with all their might. I cheered with them, though I confess I scarcely knew for what...

...the din of battle continued. Grape and canister shot were pouring through our port-holes like leaden rain... The large shot came against the ship's side like iron hail, shaking her to the very keel, or passing through her timbers and scattering terrific splinters, which did more appalling work than even their own death-giving blows... What then with splinters, cannon-balls, grape and canister poured incessantly upon us ... the work of death went on...'

A 40-man prize crew was put on board *Sabina* under Lieutenants Culverhouse and Hardy and she was taken in tow. The prize crew, which included Samuel, were all picked men. *Blanche*, some distance away, had also beaten her opponent *Ceres* in a straight fight and was about to board her. It seemed as though it was going to be a repetition of the double single-ship fight between *Dido* and *Minerve* and *Lowestoft* and *Artémise* in June, 1795.

Nelson sat down to write his report to Admiral Jervis, but soon had to break off as more Spanish ships came in sight, as a result of which *Blanche* had to abandon her attempted boarding of *Ceres*, and she escaped. The first of the new arrivals, the *Matilda* (34), was easily seen off by *la Minerve* but, next morning at dawn, a Spanish frigate appeared, followed by two line-of-battle ships, including the 112-gun *Pricipe-de-Asturias*, and Nelson was forced to instruct Cockburn to abandon his prize.

The loss of the prize must have cost Samuel dear. With their prize money, seamen on a frigate could, on an average cruise, expect to double their wages. These, unlike in the army, had not increased since 1658 and stood at £14.62 for an A.B., £11.37 for Ordinary Seamen and £10.57 for 'landsmen', less deductions for the Naval Hospital, the 'Chatham Chest' (a pension fund), the ship's surgeon and the chaplain. A contemporary cartoon 'Equity or a Sailor's Prayer before Battle' prays that the enemy's shot may be shared between officers and men in the same proportions as prize money. After the Nore mutiny in 1797 wages and conditions were improved, as was the proportion of any prize money that went to the lower ranks.

More painful than the loss of their prize, Nelson also had to abandon Culverhouse, Hardy and the prize crew on *Sabina* and run for it, as both *Minerve* and *Blanche* were themselves in no condition to fight, let alone take on a superior force, both British frigates having suffered a fair amount of damage in the previous night's action. Nelson had started off his report on a high note but, having lost both prizes and a prize crew, was forced to end it '…an unpleasant tale'. Later, he arranged for a gold-handled sword to be made for Captain Cockburn to mark the occasion, which is now in the National Maritime Museum at Greenwich.

This was the action for which Samuel won the first clasp to his Naval General Service medal. Poor Samuel, he had to spend Christmas in a Spanish jail (or, more probably, in the airless hold of a Spanish

Samuel Blackmore's Naval General Service medal, with three clasps.

ship) along with Culverhouse, Hardy and 39 other shipmates. His reward for being away from his ship under these circumstances, as one might expect from the primitive accounting system then in use, was the loss of his wages for his six weeks absence from the ship's muster! However, overall he seemed to have done pretty well financially (presumably because of his share of the prize money) as he was sometimes able to send home, via the cumbersome naval accounting system, sums in excess of a year's wages.

Marshall's Naval Biography gives us this summary of the encounter;

> 'The Spanish Captain had hardly been conveyed aboard *la Minerve* when the *Matilda*, of 34 guns, came up, compelled to cast off the prize and brought her to action. After half an hour's trial of strength, the British frigate compelled this her second antagonist to wear and haul off, and would most probably have captured her, had not a 3-decker and two other ships hove in sight. The *Blanch* [sic] … was far to windward, and *la Minerve* escaped only by the anxiety of the enemy to recover their own ship, in which they succeeded…'

There are many detailed reports of the *Sabina* affair, but Nelson's own official report, reproduced in the London Gazette, gives the best account of the part played by Culverhouse, Hardy and the prize crew on *Sabina*;

> '…Lieutenants Culverhouse and Hardy, with a proper number of men, being put in charge of the *Sabina*, and she taken in tow at four AM, a frigate was seen coming up, which by her signals, was known to be Spanish. At half past four she came to action with the *Minerve*, which cast off her prize, and Lieutenant Culverhouse was directed to stand to the southward; after a trial of strength of more than half an hour, she wore and hauled off, and I am confident she would have shared the fate of her companion. At this time three other ships were seen standing for the *Minerve*; hope was alive that they were only frigates, and also that the *Blanche* was one of them; but when the day dawned it was mortifying to see they were two Spanish ships of the line and two frigates, and the *Blanche* far to windward … it required all the skill of Captain Cockburn … to get off with a crippled ship: And here I must also do justice to Lieutenants Culverhouse and Hardy, and express my tribute of praise in their management of the prize; a frigate repeatedly fired into her without effect, and at last the Spanish Admiral quitted the pursuit of the *Minerve* for that of the *Sabina*, who was steering a different course, evidently with the intention of attracting the notice of the Admiral, as English colours were hoisted over the Spanish. The *Sabina's* main and foremasts fell overboard before she surrendered.'

Nelson also publicly recognised that the conduct of the action had, in fact, been Cockburn's;

'The enemy frequently within shot by bringing up the breeze, it required the skill of captain Cockburn, which he eminently displayed, to get off with a crippled ship.'

He was equally magnanimous about Culverhouse's attempts on the captured *Sabina* to draw the Spaniards away from *la Minerve*, by flying the British flag over the Spanish flag. It is likely that, without his help in this manner, *Minerve* herself would have been captured and, with her, Nelson;

'...the most strenuous union of coolness and seamanship' was displayed by Culverhouse and his prize crew on *Sabina*, who harried the Spaniards until her remaining masts went overboard 'and she lay a mere wreck on the water'.

Had Nelson been captured, what course would history itself have taken? It is a stroke of luck that, not only was the action well written up and documented on account of Nelson's own involvement, but one of the handful of personal accounts of life on the lower deck in the Royal Navy in Nelson's day that have come down to us (discovered in America in the 1980s) was written by Jacob Nagle, an American who was, at that time, an A.B. on *Blanche*. His graphic account[65] of the engagement, complete with his own unique spelling which has been faithfully reproduced here, was written from memory some years later and differs in point of detail from other accounts;

'We ware sent over to Leghorn for cattle, which we could get by smuglin off in the night, along shore, and likewise fresh beef, though the French had possession. In returning ... we saw a very great elumenation towards the island of Cossaco [Corsica] but could not emagin wat it might be, but when arriving in the bay we ware inform'd a French three-decker that had been taken by the English was burnt to the waters edge. We wnt out again ... and went to Elbo [Elba], which had been taken by Nelson, and we wnt to that port where Com'd Nelson was then lying in the *Manerva* Frigate.

'We ware then ordered to join the fleet ... Jervice and his fleet sailed for Giberalter, and we joined them ... but the night before we got into Giberalter we fell foul of the admiral ship [HMS *Victory*] and carried away her fore yard without doing any damage to ourselves.

'The fleet under Jarvis went off Cadis and blockaded the Spanish fleet, which was laying there. Nelson in the *Manerva* Frigate was ordered up the Straits again to the island of Elbow to convoy the transports and troops down to Jiberalter. We sailed with a pleasant breeze in the after noon. Sailing a long the Spanish shore we fell in with a Spanish coaster running a long the

---

65 'The Nagle Journal: A diary of the Life of Jacob Nagle, Sailor, from the Year 1775 to 1841' edited by John C Dann, published by Weidenfeldt & Nicholson, New York, 1988.

Spanish shore. We brought her two and boarded hur. She was loaded with bales of silk, but overhalling hur log book we found there was two Spanish frigates crusing off Cathergeen. Nelson ordered 7 bails of silk to be hoisted out of hur for a drink for the sailors and let hur go... As the *Manerve* that he was in was the faster sailer, he kept a stern. Nelson gave orders as soon as we should sea the frigates to heave two till he came up.

'It had now been dark a considerable time. At lengh we spied a sail a head laying two, and we hove two till Nelson came up and spoke, as by this time we purceived the other a beam of us with a top light. Nelson stood for the commedore ship [the *Santa Sabina*] and we for the other [*Ceres*]. Before we got to our antagonist Nelson was a long side of the commedore and poared a broad side into hur and killed 36 men on the quarter-deck, beside the capt, first and second leutenant, beside what was slaughtered on the main deck and forecastle. The third leutenant made an atemps to fight hur, but in vain. They struck and Nelson took possession and put 30 men on board and took hur in tow. Nelsons ship mounted 36 guns and the Spanish ship 48.

'In the *Blanche* we ware not idel. We run as close along side as we could without running on board of hur and gave hur a broadside fore and aft. We played so hot upon them, they run from there quarters. The second broadside we shot ahead and laying a cross hur bows, raked hur for and aft and carried away hur fore topgall and royal stays. Rounding two under hur lee, we gave hur another broadside. Hur topsails and colours all came down by the run. When they did fire there guns they ware in such haste that there shot all went over us.

We ware boarding hur when we spied a 74 gun ship and two frigates close a board. We up boat and made sail. We hall'd our wind, having the weather gage.[66] They all stood for Nelson. He, having the frigate in tow and seeing the 74 close on board, cut and run, at the same time gave the seventy four a broadside, and the 30 men on bd the prize gave hur a broad side and then struck.[67] When taking possession they all gave chace after Nelson.

We huging the wind ... they supposed us to belong to the convoy which we new nothing of till daylight, when we found our selves in the midst of a fleet of merchant men... Nelson then made signals to us, but we dared not answer them. We remained quietly till night, then droping our side of the fleet and stood over for the Turkish shore... By that means we escaped, for

---

66 i.e. they were to windward, and could therefore dictate events. 'Hauled our wind' means they pointed the ship up into the wind in order to slow her down or stop her.

67 i.e. hauled down her colours to signify surrender. To surrender without a token fight, even against overwhelming odds, was considered a court martial offence. Equally, to save unnecessary loss of life, there was no dishonour in surrendering once a reasonable fight had been put up.

we ware out of trim and could not sail as she generally had done. Nelson out ran them all excepting one small frigate that could come up with him, but he got two long 18 pounders out of the gun room ports and two more out of the cabin windows[68] and two on the quarter-deck, which was 6 long eighteens. When she would come about half gun shot, he would bore hur fore and aft. She would then drop a stern. By that means he escaped and got into the island of Elbow three days before us, which made him doubtful but what we ware taken. When we came to an anchor Nelson came on board and ordered the capt to beat to quarters, and as we ware in a line before the guns, he came round the decks and shook hands with us as he went along and telling us he was rejoice'd to find that we had escaped.[69]

The 30 man that had been taken was carried into Cathejene and the Spanierde treated them well and sent them back and Nelson returned there prisoners. They gave an account: the frigate that we engaged was brought in by two frigates, slung with harsers,[70] one frigate on each side to keep hur from sinking. The day before they took an English transport and those men were on board at the time we engaged them. They said the Spanish officers run several men through with their swords, driving them to their quarter.'

When the day was over, Nelson wrote to Jervis, his Commander-in-Chief;

'You, Sir, are so thoroughly acquainted with the merits of Captain Cockburn, that it is needless for me to express them; but the Discipline of *la Minerve* does the highest credit to her Captain and Lieutenants, and I wish fully to declare the sense I entertain of their judgment and gallantry. Lieutenant Culverhouse is an old officer of distinguished merit. Lieutenants Hardy, Gage, and Noble, deserve every praise which gallantry and zeal justly entitled them to, as does every other officer and man in the ship.'

Pushing on for Elba, *Minerve* made temporary repairs to her damage at sea, and

---

68 In January 1795, the *Blanche* had fought and won a duel with the *Pique* (36) during which she needed to fire her heavy guns rearwards. But she had no stern ports where needed; presumably this would have been on the lower deck (in the gunroom, as the wardroom of a frigate was called) as the stern windows in the captain's cabin on the upper deck, the 'gun deck,' were easily dismountable. So the first lieutenant (the captain having just then been killed) rapidly decided to make a couple of stern-facing ports in the quickest manner he could think of – he shot two of his 12-pounder long guns through his own stern, with firemen standing by with fire buckets to put out the resulting fire.

69 Nelson's style of leadership, well illustrated by this incident which shows his relationship with the men under his command, was almost unknown until World War II.

70 Nagle, an American, seems to have picked up an English west-country accent. His spelling of 'hawser' suggests Samuel would have pronounced it 'Darset' rather than 'Dorset'. If current American English is a guide, he would probably also have called a mooring buoy a 'booey'.

luckily had done so by 24 December when she chased and captured the *Maria* (6 guns and 68 crew) which was taken in tow with an officer and eight men on her as a prize crew. Samuel, of course, was absent from his ship when the *Maria* was taken and therefore would not have shared in her value as a prize.

Nelson wrote to Jervis pointing out that *Minerve* was now nearly 90 men below establishment,

> 'although I have some hopes that those taken in the prize may be returned to Gibraltar; they are all good men … my coxswain, an invaluable man is also a prisoner. If you can, pray Sir, procure some good men for Cockburn.'

On 27 December *La Minerve* arrived at Porto Ferrajo, on the island of Elba, ahead of *Blanche* and found the English community getting ready for a ball, which Nelson was invited to attend; to his embarrassment, the orchestra struck up 'Hail the Conquering Hero Comes'. He had difficulties with the army who, although Nelson had written orders to bring them off, refused point blank to move without a written order from the army!

At Porto Ferrajo, *Minerve* had to have both her main and mizzen masts replaced – an indication of the sorry shape she was in. Whilst she was being repaired, Nelson penned a letter to Don Miguel Gaston, Captain General of the Department of 'Carthagene' (the Spanish commander at Cartagena) about Hardy and the forty men he had been forced to abandon. Polite and respectful, as always, when addressing a Spaniard, he wrote;

'His Britannic Majesty's Ship the *Minerve*, at sea

Sir,   December 24th, 1796

'The fortune of war put *la Sabina* into my possession after she had been most gallantly defended; the same fickle Dame returned her to you with some of my officers and men in her.

'I have endeavoured to make the captivity of Don Jacobo Stuart, her brave commander, as light as possible; and I trust to the generosity of your nation for its being reciprocal for the British officers and men. I consent, Sir, that Don Jacobo may be exchanged and at full liberty to serve his King when Lieutenants Culverhouse and Hardy are delivered into the garrison of Gibraltar with such others as may be agreed on by the cartel established between Gibraltar and St Roche, for the exchange of prisoners.

'I have also a domestic taken in *La Sabina*, his name is Israel Coulson. Your Excellency will, I am sure, order him to be immediately restored to me, for which I will consider myself to be obliged to you.

'I also trust that those men, now prisoners of war with you, will be sent to Gibraltar. It becomes great nations to act with generosity to each other, and to soften the horrors of war.

I have the honour to be, with the most perfect esteem,

Your most obedient servant,

HORATIO NELSON'

The Spaniards were glad to agree to exchange Culverhouse, Hardy and their prize crew for Don Jacob, who was sent back under a flag of truce. At the same time, Nelson wrote to his commanding officer, Admiral Don Juan Marino;

'I cannot allow Don Jacobo to return to you without expressing my admiration of his gallant conduct. To you, who have seen the state of his ship, it is needless to mention the impossibility of her longer defence. I have lost many brave men: but, in our masts, I was most fortunate; or, probably, I should have had the honour of your acquaintance. But it pleased God to order it otherwise, for which I am thankful.'

Whilst the two frigates were at Elba, an event occurred that must have been witnessed by all on board *Minerve*, and sent her buzzing – probably still buzzing when Samuel was released from captivity and rejoined his ship in February and heard the news.

The background deserves an explanation. Many Englishmen feared that the spirit of the French Revolution would spread to England. Civil unrest at home (or the fear of it) was rife throughout this period. At Exmouth, Samuel Blackmore's home town in Devon, as elsewhere, there were bread riots. Many joined the Volunteers to help maintain order. Trewman's Exmouth Flying Post for 24 November 1796 records the burial of Samuel's brother;

'George Blackmore, whitesmith aged 21, being one of Capt. Coleridge's Company of Exmouth Volunteers, nearly the whole of which Company attended the funeral, where a most excellent sermon was delivered, after which the Corps was interred with military honours.'

Civil unrest increased with the invasion threat. On 16 April 1801 this Declaration appeared, to which James Blackmore, fifer (Samuel's cousin) added his signature;

'We, the Officers, Non-Commissioned Officers and Privates of the 2nd Exmouth Company of Volunteers, do publicly declare our determined resolution to supporting the Civil Power in suppressing Riots and Tumults and standing forward in defense of the laws of our Country agreeably to the Oath we have taken.'

The increasing threat of invasion sent men flocking in droves to join the Volunteers. By 1804, with invasion fever at its height, 380,000 men had joined. Although some political opponents of the Volunteer movement doubted their value as a fighting force, Lord Wyndham (Secretary for War) saying they were 'painted cherries which none but simple birds would take for real fruit', official reports (backed up by Lord Cornwallis) said they were fit to stand alongside the regular army. But the reference to painted cherries was not without foundation. The officers wore the King's uniform and carried the King's commission. 'Scarlet fever' went to some of their heads;

> 'indulging themselves in costly regimentals, uniforms often extravagant and impractical, with sashes and cross-belts, and head-dress of every description, including cocked hats with turbans of scarlet silk or moleskin, and bearskins decorated with cockades, gilt ornaments, badges and feathers.'[71]

Unrest in the Royal Navy had also been growing alarmingly. A number of petitions from sailors demanding the redress of their grievances had been received by the Admiralty during 1796, not only seeking better pay, food and conditions, but also demanding that unjust officers should be dismissed. Hardly surprisingly, this led to the Nore and Spithead mutinies in the spring of 1797. They were odd affairs. Officers were merely put on shore; only a few at the Nore were killed. Major ships entering the Thames were called upon to surrender and join the mutineers and those ignoring the warning were fired upon but, in typical British fashion, the gunners managed to miss. As to the French, the mutineers promised that, if Napoleon's invasion forces sailed, the whole fleet would put to sea immediately. The Spithead mutiny was handled promptly and well, and was soon over, but the Nore was led by rabble-rousers and was more serious. The men had many grievances, most of them fully justified, but, surprisingly, discipline and punishment did not feature in their list.

The crew of *Blanche* had themselves written a letter to the Admiralty in December 1795; the man elected to write[72] it was no doubt chosen by his shipmates because of his skills with pen and paper!

> 'A Humble petition on a Count of Ill Usage in the first place we are imployd from morning to two or three of Clock the after noon in washing and Scrubing the Dicks and Every Day ower Chest and Bags is Ordered on Dick and not Down till night nor Our selves neither Even so particler as to wash

---

71 Brian Southam, 'Jane Austen and the Navy.' 2001.
72 Samuel probably couldn't read or write. His brother John could; like his father, he was parish clerk at Littleham. When it was discovered that Nagle could write he thought he was going to be in trouble. Instead he was promoted 'clerk'.

the Dicks with fresh Water and if we gate wett at any time and hang or spread our Cloas to drip our captain thros them overboard by which we Big the favour of another Commander or an other Ship we still Remain your most Worthy Subjects

Blanches

Crew'

In June 1796 *Blanche's* captain, Sawyer, had been caught ordering young sailors to his hammock – 'Capt Sawyer, having a fondness for young men and boys...' as Nagle put it in his 'Journal'. This became generally known. He had also let discipline fall to an all-time low by allowing insubordination by his coxswain Mullins (one of those whom he had taken to his cabin) who had openly called him 'a man fucking bugger' and had accused him of having 'frig'd' and been 'frig'd' by two midshipman and by John Friday, a black seaman, as a result of which he virtually lost control of his ship. The First Lieutenant wrote to Nelson demanding a Court Martial, but Sawyer refused to forward the letter. Sawyer brought counter-charges against him and most of the other officers. Cockburn himself became involved, and produced letters to the court from Sawyer in which he convicted himself. On 18 October 1796 he was dismissed.

Sawyer was temporarily replaced by a junior captain, Captain D'Arcy Preston. In January 1797, Preston was transferred by Nelson to HMS *Dido*, the ship that had captured *la Minerve* from the French in 1795. To the horror of *Blanche's* crew, Preston's replacement was to be Henry Hotham, the nephew of the admiral whom Nelson so despised for signalling 'Return to Fleet' just as *Agamemnon* had been about to take *Ça Ira* in 1795.

The crew of *Blanche*, according to Jacob Nagle, knew Captain Hotham to be a strict disciplinarian;[73]

> '...bearing the name of such a tarter by his own ship's crew... That our ship mutinized and entirely refused him. He came on board [7 January 1797], had the officers armed on the quarter-deck and all hands turned aft to hear his commission read at the capstain head. They all cried out "No, no, no." He asked them what they had to say against. One of the petty officers replyed that his ships company informed us that he was a dam'd tarter and we would not have him and went forward and turned the two forecastle guns aft with canester shot.

---

[73] Not as bad as Prince William who, given his first command and despised by his men for his dissolute life and the unpleasant diseases he had contracted, decreed that the use of the word 'bugger' would bring down severe punishment!

'He then went in his boat on board [Nelson's ship] and returned with the com first leutenant. When on bd he ordered all hands aft. He called all the petty officers out and pareded them in a line on the quarter deck. "Now, my lads, if you resist Taking Capt Hotham as your capt, every third man shall be hung." The crew flew in a body forward to the guns with match[74] in hand, likewise crowbars, handspikes, and all kinds of weapons they could get holt of and left him, Capt Hotham, and the officers standing looking at us. They consulted for a moment and returned on bd Commodore Nelson. [i.e. *la Minerve*.]

'In the space of half an hour the Commodore came on bd, called all hands aft, and enquired the reason of this disturbance. He was inform'd of Capt Hotham's character, which was the reason that we refused him.

"Lads", said he, "you have the greatest caracter on bd the *Blanche* of any frigates crew in the Navy. You have taken two frigates supperiour to the frigate you are in, and now to rebel. If Capt Hotham ill treats you, give me a letter and I will support you."

'Amediately there was three chears given and Capt Hotham shed tears, and Nelson went on bd of his ship.'

Although he disliked unnecessary punishments, Nelson was in fact a strict disciplinarian. Had this episode cropped up after the events at the Nore and Spithead later that year, he would without any doubt have hanged the ringleaders from *Blanche's* yard-arm.

When Jacob Nagle was serving later as prize-master on the sloop *Netley* he says that, rather than flog a man, her captain devised alternative punishments which seem to have worked;

'Captain Bond took a delight in making his ships company comfortable, and when in harbour as much liberty as could be expected. He could not bare to punish men at the gangway, but he contrived a collar of one inch plank to ware round there necks with a large padlock for any certain time, which they dreaded more than flogging. Likewise for greater crimes was a scarlot cap full of black tossles hung all over it. When any strangers came on board, those men that had them on would sneak a way below for shame.'

Cockburn, too (in later life, at least) came to dislike unnecessary floggings, and wrote congratulatory notes to his captains if they had managed to avoid using the 'cat' in their punishment reports. When, in America in the 1812 war, he recruited deserting negro slaves into the Marines, defaulters (who were very

---

[74] This suggests that *Blanche* still had the older cannons which were fired by holding a 'linstock' (a smouldering rope) to the touch-hole, rather than the new flintlock mechanism.

proud of their smart new scarlet Marine uniform jackets and white pipe-clay belts) were made to wear their beloved jackets inside-out.

The same cannot be said of Hardy, described as 'tall, dour, heavily built'. It sounds as though he was an out-and-out bully. *Victory's* log shows that, two days after Trafalgar, he gave two men three dozen lashes each for drunkenness, and during the 18 months prior to Trafalgar, whilst Hardy was captain of *Victory*, he ordered 308 floggings. Three of the men had 200 lashes each for desertion (probably whilst on shore on a watering party) which was technically punishable by death, the men being 'flogged round the fleet'. Tied to a frame erected in one of the ship's boats, they were each given 50 lashes in front of *Victory's* crew, who were all assembled to 'witness punishment', and then 50 more in front of the crews of three other ships. These unfortunate men, who may not all have lived long enough to savour all 200 strokes of the 'cat', would have been sentenced by a court martial, consisting of the captains of other ships, but most of the other floggings were ordered by Hardy himself.

Whilst *la Minerve* was being repaired, Nelson sent his friend Captain Freemantle in *Inconstant* to Naples to bring back the former Viceroy of Corsica, Sir Gilbert Elliot, and his suite. Freemantle took the opportunity of marrying Betsy Wynne whilst there, bringing her back with him on his ship. She was pretty and witty, vivacious and a natural-born hostess. There was inevitably much celebration and partying to be done on *Inconstant* and the other ships. Cockburn therefore found that he had a great deal of hospitality to repay on board his own ship, and it 'became rather a bacchanalia'.[75]

Minerve left Porto Ferajo for Gibraltar on 29 January 1797 in company with *Romulus* (Nelson having sent the rest of the squadron, with twelve transports, directly to Gibraltar by the safer southern route) and called in to see what was happening at San Fiorenzo Bay and Toulon on the way. On board, as Nelson's guests, were Sir Gilbert Elliot and his suite, including his aide-de-camp, Colonel John Drinkwater, a well-known military historian.

Nearly forty years later, in 1836, a young Lieutenant stationed in Bermuda on board HMS *President* wrote to his mother. His letter[76] mentions Sir George Cockburn and gives us a glimpse of life on board *Minerve* on the voyage back to Gibraltar, short-handed as they were without the prize crew they had lost on *Sabina*;

---

75 Pack, 'The Man who burned the White House'.
76 Devereux Papers MS/83/062 – National Maritime Museum, Greenwich.

'He … tells a good story abt. that. When he commanded some frigate not a few years ago he took Sir Gilbert Elliot from Leghorn or somewhere to Gibraltar. He and his suite insisted on being stationed to guns i.e. quartered, and at the muster at quarters [which] takes place every evening to see the ship's Co. sober etc the midshipmen mustd. Gilbert Elliot – [answered] No 1. 1st Captn. & Boarder. Pozzo di Borgo No. 2 2nd Captain etc. Much to the amusement of all hands.'

Although not material to this story, his letter goes on, in the manner of a Jane Austen novel, to mention a ball at the Admiral's;

'after one of which a young lady took it into her head she was abt. to become yr. daughter in law – at least she said to her friend who of course kept the secret by spreading it. "She was sure that I meant something, I was so very pointed in my attentions, every body remarked it, & she wondered that I did not come and call on her" & I suppose tell her a tale of love. Poor little fool.'

Minerve arrived back at Gibraltar on 9 February 1797. Next day Culverhouse, Hardy and the prize crew rejoined their ship from the Spanish ship *Terrible* (74 guns) which lay just across the bay in Spanish water, accompanied, no doubt, by much cheering, back-slapping and friendly banter from their shipmates, the log book reading;

'Friday 10th February. Moored in Gibraltar (Rosier Bay) … came on board Lieutenants Culverhouse & Hardy with the seamen taken on the Spanish Frigate 20th December 1796 of [sic] Cartagena…'

At Gibraltar Nelson learned that a large Spanish fleet had passed through into the Atlantic only four days before, with orders to join up with the French fleet and escort an armed invasion of Ireland, so it was vital to find them and prevent them from joining the French. He therefore hastened westward into the Atlantic after them as soon as the missing men were safely back on board.

Back on his own ship he may have been, but poor Samuel's troubles were not yet over. He seems to have been temporarily assigned to some other duties for ten days or so, shortly before the *Sabina* affair, and had lost his bedding roll in the process; tiresome, as he had only just bought it for 11s.4d [56p] from the ship's purser, to whom he had to apply for a replacement, for which he was debited a further 11s.4d. Worse, when taken by the Spanish on *Sabina*, he lost all his oil-skins and wet-weather gear, the replacement of which set him back £6.7s [£6.35] which was an enormous sum for an A.B. to find. Until then he had not bought any tobacco from the ship's purser, but the experience of a Spanish jail seems to have driven him to smoking (or, more likely, chewing 'quid'!) as he also ran up a bill for a further 25s.4d [£1.27] for tobacco at the same time.

Two Spanish 'ships of the line', one of them the *Terrible*, had been keeping a sharp lookout for Nelson and as soon as they saw *Minerve* put out from Gibraltar, they put out from Algeciras (opposite Gibraltar) and gave chase. Col. Drinkwater's account of what followed is based on the notes he took at the time;[77]

> 'On the afternoon of the 11th February, the *Minerve* got under weigh. She had scarcely cast around from her anchorage, when two of the three Spanish line-of-battle ships in the upper part of Gibraltar Bay were observed to be also in motion... As the Spanish ships had a steady wind from the eastward over the isthmus, whilst the *Minerve* was embarrassed with the eddies and baffling flaws ... near the Rock, the Spaniards had for some time the advantage... The *Minerve* was not, however, long in getting the steady breeze ... when the chace [sic] of the enemy became ... a most interesting "spectacle" to our friends in the garrison.

> 'The *Minerve* was ... considered to be a tolerably good sailer, particularly with the wind on her quarter. The Spaniards were not equally good goers; one of them, the *Terrible*, was a first-rate sailer, well known to the British officers, Culverhouse and Hardy, who had been exchanged from her only the day before ... the *Minerve* had the wind abaft, and marking her progress with that of the enemy, it was evident that the headmost ship of the chace gained on the British frigate. No sooner was this ascertained, than directions were given by Sir Gilbert Elliott [sic] to have certain parts of his public papers ready to be sunk, if necessary, at a moment's notice. The ship was cleared for action, and the position of the *Minerve* was now becoming every moment more and more interesting.'

Cockburn saw that the Spanish seemed to be gaining on them and ordered the studding sails to be set. Looking at the Spanish ships pursuing them, and noting *Minerve* being cleared for action, Col Drinkwater asked Nelson if he thought that an engagement was likely. Nelson replied that it was very possible but, pointing to his personal pendant at the mast-head, he said;

> 'Before the Don gets hold of that bit of bunting, I will have a struggle with them, and sooner than give up the Frigate I'll run her ashore'.[78]

At this point, according to Drinkwater, dinner was announced and the officers of *Minerve* and their guests then sat down to dinner. Col Drinkwater, sitting next to Hardy, congratulated him on his escape from captivity, and was hoping to hear the story of his capture, when the cry 'Man overboard' went up. William

---

[77] His book 'A Narrative of the Battle of St. Vincent' was re-published in 1969, oddly enough by William R Blackmore.

[78] 'Ashore' was only used for ships going aground; men went 'on shore'.

Barnes, a seaman working on *Minerve's* sails, had fallen into the water. Hardy leaped from the table and the dinner party broke up. Drinkwater's account continues;

'The officers of the ship ran on deck; I, with others, ran to the stern-windows to see if anything could be observed of the unfortunate man; we had scarcely reached them before we noticed the lowering of the jolly-boat, in which was my neighbour, Hardy, with a party of sailors; and before many seconds had elapsed, the current of the Straights had carried the jolly-boat far astern of the Frigate, towards the Spanish ships. Of course, the first object was to recover the fallen man, but he was never seen again. Hardy soon made a signal to that effect, and the man was given up for lost. The attention of every person was now turned to the safety of Hardy and his boat's crew; their situation was extremely perilous, and their danger was every instant increasing, from the fast sailing of the headmost ship of the chase, which by this time had approached nearly within gun-shot of the *Minerve*. The jolly-boat's crew pulled 'might and main' to regain the Frigate, but apparently made little progress against the current of the Straights. At this crisis, Nelson, casting an anxious look at the hazardous situation of Hardy and his companions, exclaimed 'By G-, I'll not lose Hardy; back the mizzen topsail.' No sooner said than done; the *Minerve's* progress was retarded, having the current carry her down toward Hardy and his party, who, seeing this spirited manoeuvre … naturally redoubled their actions to rejoin the Frigate.

'To the landsmen on board the *Minerve* an action now appeared to be inevitable; and so, it would appear, thought the Enemy, who surprised and confounded by this daring manoeuvre of the Commodore (being ignorant of the accident that led to it), must have construed it into a direct challenge. Not conceiving, however, a Spanish Ship of the Line to be an equal match for a British frigate, with Nelson on board of her, the captain … suddenly shortened sail, in order to allow his consort to join him, and thus afforded time for the *Minerve* to drop down to the jolly-boat to take out Hardy and the crew; and the moment they were on board the Frigate, orders were given again to make sail. Being now under studding sails, and the widening of the Straits allowing the wind to be brought more on the *Minerve's* quarter, the Frigate soon regained the lost distance, and at sunset, by steering further to the southward, we lost sight of him and his consort altogether.'

A ship's log, almost entirely concerned with wind and sea, and often quite unmoved by great events, is less likely to give a full picture than an on-the-spot record by a noted military historian. But why should it not record the truth on points of detail? Here is the log for that day;

"By God I'll not lose Hardy; back the mizzen topsail" by Sue Simpson

'Sunday February 12th.1797

"...Fresh Gales & hazy Wea^r. At ¼ pst 3 Wm Barnes Seaman fell over board, hove to & lowered the Jolly Boat down but could not save him. ½ pst 3 hoisted [?the] Boat in. 2 Line of Battle (Spanish) Ships being in Chase of us which had Cut or Slip'd from Algizeras [sic]. Dist. about 3 Miles, made all sail, At 8 made & shortened Sail Occasionally, Cape Spartel ESE Dist. 4 Leag^s....'

Was *Terrible* as much as three miles away? Was *Minerve* fully 'hove to', or did Nelson (or was it Cockburn who, as captain, had command of the ship?) order only the mizzen topsail to be backed in order to take some, not all, of the way off the ship? Did a good story, as seen through a land-lubber's eyes, improve with the telling?

As we shall see, Samuel later became Coxswain of *la Minerve*, which means he must have by then acquired considerable experience of small boat work. To gain this, it is likely that one of his duties had been to pull an oar in one of the ship's boats. He may even have been one of those who manned the jolly boat on this occasion.

Drinkwater, a 'landsman', misunderstood the effect of the strong eastward current through the Straights of Gibraltar – all three participants in this drama, the *Minerve*, her jolly-boat and the leading Spanish battle ship were, of course, *equally* effected by the current. Their relative positions would therefore not have been in the least affected by it. But, IF Drinkwater's account was entirely accurate, it must have been a close-run thing as, even if *Minerve* herself was not quite within gunshot range, the jolly-boat would have been. It would only have presented a minimal target, however, and was probably considered by the Spanish to be literally not worth powder and shot. But was the log book perhaps more accurate?

CHAPTER 5

That night there was a thick mist. Sir Gilbert and Col Drinkwater were sleeping in Nelson's cabin. When he came in, Drinkwater awoke and asked Nelson what was happening. He told him they were in the middle of either a Spanish convoy heading for the West Indies, or the entire Spanish fleet. Drinkwater woke Sir Gilbert, a heavy sleeper, to tell him of the situation; all he said was 'We are only passengers, and must submit to circumstances' and promptly went back to sleep.

Captain Cockburn sailed *Minerve* silently straight through the middle of the Spanish fleet which Nelson had been looking for. Gradually edging away from the Spaniards, he cleared their fleet and then hastened to rejoin Admiral Jervis and the rest of the British fleet. Nelson found Jervis and the fleet (15 ships of the line, including Samuel's old ship *Diadem*) off Cape St Vincent on 13 February 1797 and straight away reported to Jervis and warned him of the approaching Spaniards. He took Culverhouse and Hardy across to *Victory* with him; their account of the Spanish fleet's morale and state of readiness (which they had only recently witnessed first-hand) comforted Jervis greatly. Nelson then said goodbye to the officers and men of *la Minerve* and went back onto his own ship *Captain*. He had in the meantime been promoted rear admiral, but this news had not yet reached the fleet.

Midshipman Parsons describes the background to the Battle of Cape St Vincent and the numerical superiority of the Spanish fleet;[79]

> 'Sir John decided, like a brave man, to fight and leave the event to Infinite Wisdom... On the 10th of February, the signal to clear for action announced the commander-in-chief's intention to fight against all odds... I remember the care used in taking down the admiral's bulkheads, and the removal of all the furniture he could do without, below. The substitution of canvas, and the open, clear appearance of the long line of guns, which now were more frequently exercised, all assumed a more martial appearance, and the round, laughing, unintellectual countenance assumed a sharpened and eager look. On the 13th, *La Minerve*, bearing the broad pendant of Commodore Sir Horatio Nelson, came down the Mediterranean, and joined the fleet.'

---

[79] 'Nelsonian Reminiscences' by Lieutenant G S Parsons RN edited by W H Long, Chatham Publishing, 1998.

Parsons adds a footnote about *Minerve*;

> 'Commanded by that gallant officer, Sir George Cockburn, whose discipline and activity were the admiration of the fleet, and often induced Sir John Jervis to treat his friends by signalising the *Minerve* to chase. The way in which she spread her canvas seemed magical.'

Jervis was planning to send the frigate *Lively* home immediately after the coming battle so, on *Minerve* rejoining the fleet, her guests, Col Drinkwater and Sir Gilbert Elliot, were transferred to *Lively*. They had requested permission to remain on *Victory* so that they could see the coming battle, but Jervis refused to allow this as it would have been much too dangerous.

Nelson's news was comforting to Jervis and confirmed his suspicion that the Spanish fleet was on its way. He had stationed himself off Cape St Vincent to block their path back to Cadiz, and now knew he was right. Before sunset on 13 February the fleet were ordered to prepare for battle and to stay in close order. The evening of 13 February saw feverish but well-drilled activity throughout the fleet. Here we have Parsons' eye-witness account again;

> 'grinding cutlasses, sharpening pikes, flinting pistols, among the boarders; filling powder and fitting well-oiled gunlocks on our immense artillery by the gunners, slinging our lower yards with chains; and, in short, preparing a well-organised first-rate for this most important battle. The men and officers seemed to me to look taller, and the anticipation of victory was legibly written on each brow.'

As the wind dropped that evening, the men waiting for the engagement heard the signal guns of the unsuspecting Spanish war ships, and this continued throughout the night as they drew nearer. That night, *Minerve* was assigned to shadow the enemy and signal their position and course back to *Culloden* which was in the van of the fleet. Parsons records the dawning of that fateful day;

> 'During the long night of the 13th February, we heard many heavy guns to wind-ward, and felt perfectly certain that they proceeded from the Spanish fleet, which could not be very remote. The day dawned in the east, and "Up all hammocks, ahoy!" resounded through the decks of His Majesty's ship *Barfleur*. Some were sent aloft to barricade the tops, while the remainder were stowed with unusual care as a bulwark round the upper decks....General signal flying on board the *Victory* for the fleet to make all sail....our two frigates and *la Bonne Citoyenne* sloop, under press of sail, to windward. At nine, the latter made the signal for a strange fleet to wind-ward....These intimations of approaching battle were received by the British squadron with reiterated cheers; and so beautifully close was our order of

sailing, that the flying jib-boom of the ship astern projected over the taffrail of the leader…'

As dawn broke on the morning of 14 February, the look-out men at the mast-heads of every ship in the fleet searched the horizon for the enemy. The day began in earnest at 6.30 when *Culloden's* signal to Jervis that five sail were seen to the south west by west was soon confirmed by the frigates *Lively* and *Niger*. The sloop *Bonne Citoyenne* was sent to reconnoitre and at 9.30 signalled back that there were eight. Half an hour later *la Minerve* signalled there were 20, followed a few minutes later by eight more, and *Bonne Citoyenne* reported that 25 of them were ships of the line. Soon they were visible to the entire fleet.

We can easily imagine the excitement mounting on all the ships there, including *la Minerve,* at the prospect of the approaching battle. Parsons recalls the scene on the flagship;

> 'I have a glimpse through the fog of their leeward line' called Signal-Lieutenant Edghill, from the mainyard, 'and they loom like Beachy Head in a fog. By my soul, they are thumpers, for I distinctly make out *four* tier of ports in one of them, bearing an admiral's flag.'

> 'Don Cordova, in the *Santissima Trinidad,*' said the vice-admiral; 'and I trust to Providence that we shall reduce this mountain into a mole hill before sunset.'

Midshipman William Hoste, one of Nelson's favourites, describes the orders from the quarter-deck being shouted round his ship, 'Up hammocks', the order to roll the hammocks up as tightly as possible and stow them in the netting round the upper deck as a protection from musket balls and flying splinters. 'Sauve-tete' netting was stretched across the deck and 'waist' of the ship to protect those below from falling spars and rigging. The galley fire was put out. All moveable bulkheads and partitions, and gun-room and dining-room tables and furniture, were also dismounted and secured. Some were put in the ship's boats (which were unshipped from the beams above the upper gun deck and towed astern or even cast adrift) to minimise the risk from flying splinters. Any self-respecting crew could 'clear for action' in six minutes – and, in a well-trained crew, all this was carried out in strict silence. Both officers and men put on clean clothing to minimise the risk of infection in the event of being wounded but, whereas most of the officers would have put on their best uniforms, 'the People' went bare-foot and mostly stripped to the waist.

The numerical odds were stacked heavily against him, but Jervis had only that week received reinforcements and morale generally was exceptionally high.

Nelson said;

> 'Of all the fleets I ever saw, I never beheld one in point of officers and men equal to Sir John Jervis', who is a commander-in-chief able to lead them to glory.'

Jervis himself knew full well the vital importance of winning. The thought of the Spanish fleet beating him, joining up with the French at Brest and landing an invasion army in Ireland was unthinkable. Besides, being forcibly ejected from the Mediterranean had hurt him deeply and dejected the whole nation; public morale, unlike that in his fleet, was at an all-time low; 'A victory is essential to England at this moment', he said.

That year, to the public's dismay, a French squadron with 15,000 soldiers on board did indeed manage to slip out of Brest during a storm and headed for Ireland, whilst the British blockade ships had taken refuge at Spithead. They reached Bantry Bay but, for three weeks, the wind was against them and they could not get in. Luckily, they were eventually forced to give up and were driven back to Brest by the storm. A considerable number from another French force did, however, land in Fishguard Bay in Wales (where the ferry terminal now is) that February, but they were soon persuaded to surrender to the local 'fencibles' and militia.

The British Navy considered itself able to take on any French or Spanish force 50 per cent. superior to itself in terms of ships, guns or men. This was not just an idle boast. Nor was it merely the uninformed bragging of the lower deck. It was a known fact. Nelson himself said;

> 'I was always of opinion, having ever acted upon it, & never having had any reason to repent, that one Englishman was equal to three Frenchmen' [80]

Experience showed that the British sailors were better trained in the vital matter of handling their guns. Although probably not more accurate, their rate of fire was far higher – and they knew it. When it came to fighting, morale was the one vital asset that the French and the Spanish fleets seldom possessed, but Jack Tar did, and in abundance. British sailors could climb the rigging in a storm, under fire if necessary, and reset the sails, as they had done it at sea a hundred times before. They could reload their heavy guns, run them out and fire them no matter how much the ship was rolling in a blow, as they had practised that at sea in rough weather a hundred times before, too. The French and Spanish were not in any way lacking in bravery, but they were kept cooped up in port. The only gun drill they did, the only setting of the sails, was on a calm sea.

---

[80] Mahan, 'The Life of Lord Nelson', vol I, p125.

The Victorian naval historian Clowes, acquitting himself in his 'Introduction' of the bias he saw in other historians, says 'In this war the French ships usually carried large but undisciplined crews and unskilled officers' and explains that this is why they usually attempted to make use of their numerical superiority by trying to board. After examining numerous single ship actions, he continues;

> 'If the shooting of the French crews was wretched – and how bad it was these actions show – the spirit and fiery courage of the French sailors – seamen we cannot call them – were above all reproach.'

At Trafalgar, the French fleet had been at sea for some months, and had plenty of time to practise their sail handling and gun drill, and they too were in no way lacking in bravery, which probably explains the terrible slaughter and damage to ships on both sides. Clowes was even less flattering about the Spanish; 'As a fighting force the Spanish navy was worthless'.

The Spaniards, like their French allies, generally fired at the British rigging and sails until they were very close, whereas the British preferred to fire heavy broadsides of round-shot straight into their hulls at close quarters, which accounted, in part, for the somewhat higher casualties that the French and Spanish ships usually suffered.

Unlike Jervis' fleet, revealed by the break of dawn to be in the two perfect parallel lines as they had practised so often before, the Spanish fleet was seen to be disorganised, scattered and split into two groups. As Jervis walked his quarter-deck, an officer with a telescope called down from the rigging;

'There are eight sail of the line, Sir John.'
'Very well, Sir.'
'There are twenty sail of the line, Sir John.'
'Very well, Sir.'
'There are twenty-five sail of the line, Sir John.'
'Very well, Sir.'
'There are twenty-seven sail of the line, Sir John – near double our own.'
'Enough, Sir, no more of that!' replied Jervis, 'The die is cast, and if there are fifty sail I will go through them. England badly needs a victory at present.'

The same information was called down from the mast-heads of every ship in the fleet for the waiting sailors to hear. The common seamens' reactions were the same as their admiral's. Quite forgetting himself in the excitement, Captain Ben Hallowell (a huge Canadian temporarily on *Victory*) thumped his admiral on the back in agreement.

As the fleets grew nearer, the marine drummer boys on every ship 'beat to quarters' and the men ran to their action stations. Red-coated marines guarded every companionway and entrance, muskets at the ready and bayonets fixed, to stop men leaving their posts. Others manned the 'fighting tops', the platforms part-way up each mast where the marines, armed with muskets, also had small brass 'swivel-guns' loaded with 'canister' (bags of musket balls) to aim at the officers on the enemy's quarter-decks.

Silence then was the primary rule, and orders for individual gun-crews were generally whispered, so that all orders from the captain could be clearly heard. Talking was strictly forbidden. The guns had their 'tompions' removed from the muzzle of the barrel, the lead 'aprons' protecting the touch-hole and firing mechanism were taken off, the gun ports were opened and the 'great guns', which until now had been lashed by the muzzle to the deck-head above, were loaded and run out. Gun-crews were busy wetting and sanding their gun decks to reduce the risk of fires from spilt gunpowder and give their feet a better grip. Down by the magazines below the water-line the powder monkeys (usually but, contrary to popular belief, not always young boys) one to each gun, were ready to scamper up and down the companionways with cartridges full of gunpowder. The surgeons in their orlop decks, painted red to disguise the inevitable pools of blood, were laying out bone saws and sharpening their probes and scalpels.

Interestingly, the reference in the Blackmore family tradition to Samuel, in later life, going on deck in his carpet-slippers may be based on fact. In a man-o'-war in action, there was always a serious fire risk on the gun decks, so shoes were banned in case an explosion was triggered by a hard nailed leather heel treading on spilt gunpowder. Seamen and gun-crews went bare-foot, of course, but officers and petty-officers working in the magazine and even on the gun decks wore over-slippers made of felt. Did Samuel acquire this habit in the Navy, and continue it all his life?

Normal fighting tactics, laid down in the Admiralty's 'Fighting Instructions', were to sail in one long line[81] along the side of the enemy, exchanging broadside for broadside. But Jervis intended to sail at right-angles to the enemy line and break through it. Divided as it was into two groups of nine and eighteen, his intended tactics seemed ideal for taking on a superior force.

The main use of a frigate in a sea battle was to act as a 'repeater'. With all the big ships in a long straight 'line of battle' it was often difficult, even at the best of times, for ships some way from the admiral's flag ship to read his flag signals. In bad weather or with gun smoke billowing from a broadside, this became

---

[81] Hence the expressions 'line of battle', 'line-of-battle ship' and 'ship of the line'.

impossible. Two or three frigates would therefore sail in a line parallel to that of the admiral's flag ship and the main battle line, repeating at their own mast-heads every flag they saw flying at the admiral's mast-head, so that all ships in the line could see his signals. In a fleet action, frigates usually only engaged other frigates and, by convention, a 'ship of the line' would not fire on a frigate unless provoked.

Repeaters might have been more use out to windward of the fleet, where their signals would not have been so badly obscured by the gun smoke. The frigates were out to windward. But Jervis' fleet had the enemy to windward, and the last thing he wanted was a line of frigates in the way. So he despatched them directly before the wind, passing astern of the 'Line of Battle', and they took up their stations to leeward of the rear of the fleet.[82]

One of the Spanish stragglers, the *San Isidro*, wore round, doubled back and passed to leeward of the British line, hoping to regain the main group of Spanish ships. She passed between the British frigates and 'the Line' as she did so. *Lively's* captain was for letting her pass, perhaps not wanting to sample her broadside, but her elderly gunner persuaded him to let him fire his favourite 18-pounder at her. Drinkwater and the others observed a hit but, as a result, she replied with a full broadside against both *Lively* and the other frigates. Luckily it was badly aimed and did no more than put a few holes in their sails. All the frigates returned her fire, but soon they were out of range.

Jervis proceeded with his plan of sailing towards the enemy and dividing them in two. However, Nelson (on board *Captain*) saw as they approached the enemy that there was a danger of the two halves of the Spanish fleet re-uniting and, on his own initiative, left the line of battle. Parsons describes Nelson's famous move;

> "The *Captain* has put her helm down,' called the signal-luff.
>
> 'Only in the wind,' said the vice-admiral; 'she will box off directly.'
>
> The admiral was wrong, and Commodore Sir Horatio Nelson went clean about, and dashed in among the Spanish van, totally unsupported, leaving a break in the British line – conduct totally unprecedented...'

Technically, to do this without any order or permission from Jervis, his commander-in-chief, was a grave breach of naval discipline. He engaged the

---

82 A more complete account of the battle, based on modern research and giving perhaps a slightly less Nelson-oriented slant than most, is to be found in the selected papers from the Battle of Cape St Vincent, Bicentennial International Naval Conference at Portsmouth, 15 February 1997 edited by Stephen Howarth and published by the Society for Nautical Research, the 1805 Club and the Nelson Society.

"Admiral Nelson receiving the Spanish Admiral's sword on board the San Josef *",*
engraved by J Rogers, c.1860

enormous four-decker *Santissima Trinidad* (130 guns) and four others of the enemy on his own until other British ships came to *Captain's* aid. Nelson then personally led a boarding party onto the *San Josef* (112 guns) and was seen dashing out along the bowsprit of his ship *Captain* close on the heels of a soldier of the 69th. He was thus second on board the *San Josef,* entering via the stern windows and brandishing his ceremonial sword.

Having secured the *San Josef,* he jumped from her onto the *San Nicolas* (80 guns) shouting 'Westminster Abbey or Victory' and took her too, accepting the surrender of her and the *San Josef's* officers' swords, thus endearing himself to both admirals and common sailors alike. They called it 'Nelson's Patent Bridge for Boarding First-Rates', or 'Nelson's New Art of Cookery' – a Spanish first-rate ship and an 80-gun ship, which were well battered and basted, without letting the fire go down, until they were 'completely dish'd, fit to set before his Majesty.' Boarding one enemy ship from another, taking both, had never been done before, let alone by an admiral in person.

Admiral Jervis himself had a near miss. The officers beside him on *Victory's* quarter-deck rushed to his aid after a cannon ball took off the head of the marine standing next to him. His whole face and chest were covered with the man's brains, blood and gore. They thought their admiral was done for too, but he was unharmed. His reaction was merely to ask a midshipman to go and fetch him an orange so that he could swill his mouth out; it must have been open at the time!

A gunner on *Goliath* at Cape St Vincent wrote;

> 'We gave them their Valentines in style; not that we loved fighting, but we all wished to be free to return home... We knew there was no other way of obtaining this than defeating the enemy. "The hotter the war, the sooner the peace," was a saying with us.'

Accounts of naval battles refer to the three tremendous cheers that Jack Tar, waiting down below on the gun decks, gave as their guns began to bear on the enemy, putting the fear of God into them. At the Battle of the Nile, Johnny Crappo (as Jack Tar called his French opposite number) on the orders of their officers, attempted a feeble reply, to be met with loud and prolonged derisory English laughter.

A frigate not acting as a 'repeater' or otherwise occupied in a fleet action was expected to take on enemy frigates and to render help to the fleet where necessary. This was the part that *Minerve* played at Cape St Vincent, fought on Valentine's Day 1797, but it was obviously not a central part. Her log book, as always, is not much help but she seems to have been in attendance upon *Captain* and directly under Nelson's orders.

During the battle, *Minerve* was ordered to take *Colossus* in tow (as her jib-boom had gone and her spars were badly damaged) and to keep her 'in station' so that her guns could still bear on the enemy. However, the offer was refused as her captain thought that other ships were in more need of assistance than he was. Instead, *Minerve* joined *Diadem* and went to help Nelson's ship *Captain* (which had also been terribly mauled) and pulled her free from an entanglement.

Having secured his two prizes, Nelson ordered *Minerve* to send a boat across to the *San Nicolas* for him. As the bow man hooked on to *Minerve's* chains and Nelson leapt up the side, his hat half shot to bits and his uniform covered in gunpowder smoke, he was received by the crew with prolonged and tumultuous cheers[83] that totally drowned the bosun's shrill and the stamp and crash of the marines as they presented arms. 'Our Nel', as he was affectionately known, was

---

83 Sir Gilbert Elliot wrote to Nelson; 'I was in hopes you were unhurt, by seeing you on board the *Minerva* [sic], and hearing the cheers you were greeted with.'

back amongst 'the Minerves' again. His Commodore's broad pendant now flying again from *Minerve's* mast-head, he was first taken to *Captain* but, finding her in rather a bad way, he asked Cockburn to take him to the first ship he could find that was still capable of fighting;

> '...who directed Captain Cockburn to proceed to the van of the British fleet, it being his intention to go on board any of the line-of-battle ships then engaged. Before this could be effected, however, the signal was made to discontinue the action; and in the evening the Commodore took up his residence on board the *Irresistible*.'[84]

Nelson had wanted to capture the totally crippled flag ship *Santissima Trinidad* which, he believed, would be his for the asking. Saumarez (captain of *Orion*) claimed, and Nelson himself confirmed, that during the battle she had in fact surrendered but, as nobody was available to board her, she had escaped when other Spanish ships came to her assistance. But the light was fading fast and, as Jervis had ordered the firing to stop, he was unable to carry out his intention.

Again, the Captain's log of *la Minerve* gives little impression of a major Fleet action;

> '...heard the report of Several Guns in the S.W.Qt^r... *Victory* ENE Dist. 3 Miles, at 6 saw 13 Sail strange Ships in the S.W Qt^r., at 7 out all Reefs, at 10 the fleet in Chase, the Spanish Fleet S.W. Dist. 5 or 6 Miles, at 20 Minutes past 11 the Van of our Fleet commenced Action with the Spanish Fleet, at Noon Fresh Breezes & hazy Wea^r, the Fleet in Close Action ... at 12 Minutes past 3 Discovd a Spanish Ship of the Line had struck her Coulours [sic], at ½ pst 5 the Fireing [sic] Ceased, when found we had taken in all 2, 3 Deck Ships, & 2 two Deckers, Wore Ship, at 10 Fleet in Comp^y, took H M Ship *Captain* in Tow...'

After the battle, *Minerve* was detailed to organise the fleet's other frigates in an attempt to tow the crippled prizes back to Lisbon, but, because of the unpredictable wind and the fact that half the Spanish fleet was still near-by and unharmed, this was thought to be impractical. So she returned to *Captain's* aid, took her in tow and sheltered her from further attack in the centre of the British fleet. Following the battle, due to the temporary absence of men who had gone to make up prize crews for the four Spanish ships taken, *Minerve's* crew fell as low as 170 men.

Lively, with Nelson's two guests on board, did not leave the fleet with her dispatches until noon on 19 February but hit strong easterly winds and did not

---

84 Marshall's Naval Biography, vol I, p 522.

arrive at Plymouth until 5 March. There, the news that the French were in the Irish Channel had thrown everyone into despair. Fear of open revolution was rife and, to cap it all, the Bank of England had suspended payment. The run on the Bank was so serious (gold being in such short supply) that Spanish dollars were issued by it on 10 March 1797, at the rate of 4s.6d [22½p] each. These were not recalled until the following October. On each coin the King's bust was struck on the Spanish King's neck, giving rise to this verse, written on *Victory* at the time;

'The additional head on the Dollar impress'd
Is to circulate Jervis's fame
To his valour 'tis owing, it must be confess'd,
England made an impression on Spain.'[85]

The economy had just about collapsed – so much so that Elliot and Drinkwater, when they landed, were only able to raise 15 guineas towards the cost of their journey to London. At first the people were incredulous, and took some convincing that they were, in fact, carrying news of the resounding victory over the Spaniards that the country so badly needed, and of the part played by Nelson in it.

Jervis' official reports reached London and, thanks to Drinkwater, so did the full story quickly gain circulation. But instead of praising him, Nelson's wife wrote him a rather petulant letter saying his antics had caused her great worry, and he should in future be more considerate of her. Unaware that it was usually the First Lieutenant's right to lead a boarding party, and that captains, commodores and admirals were meant to remain on their ships, she added that, as to leading boarding parties, 'I beg you … LEAVE IT for CAPTAINS!' Blockade duty and thrashing the Spaniards were not the only things on Nelson's mind. Fanny also wrote to him with strict instructions about his step-son Josiah, a midshipman; 'Do make him clean his teeth not cross ways but upwards and downwards'.

When Nelson's part at St Vincent became known, he was not universally acclaimed. Captain Parker claimed that Nelson had only been able to board the *San Josef* after he in the *Prince George* had already crippled her. Shortly after the battle, news of Nelson's promotion as admiral came through, and Sir John Jervis became Earl St Vincent[86].

An entry now appears in *Minerve's* muster book, all entered up in perfect copperplate handwriting, but this one has a blot on it;

---

85 Nicholson, 'Dispatches and Letters of Lord Nelson', Vol II, p363.
86 He was, in fact, created the Earl *of* St Vincent, but the Navy List got it wrong and the error has been perpetuated ever since.

'16 men from *Captain* – 15 died 17th Febry'.

An important victory had been obtained, and one that Britain badly needed, but at a price – and most of the Spanish fleet not only remained intact, but showed every sign of being capable of renewing the fight.

In fairness to the Spaniards, it must be noted that in some ways the contest was hardly an equal one. Drinkwater points out that even their flag ships had only sixty or eighty trained seamen on board, the rest being landsmen and newly levied soldiers.

> 'An officer of one of the prizes said, that ... it was impossible, after the first broadside, for the captain or officer to persuade any of the crew to go aloft to repair the injured rigging: threats and punishment were equally ineffectual. He had seen some severe examples made ... but though two or three had been killed ... the panic-struck wretches, when called upon to go aloft, fell immediately on their knees, and ... cried out, that they preferred being sacrificed on the spot, to performing a duty in the execution of which they considered death as inevitable.'

> 'On board the *San Josef* ... four or five tompions were still fixed in the quarter-deck guns of the side that had been engaged; and the reason being demanded, the people on board replied, with a shrug of the shoulders, that the animated and destructive cannonade of the British ships had not allowed them to fire these guns. It was a question, indeed, if they were loaded. It was observed also, by....the British squadron, that as soon as their guns were run out to repeat a broadside, the enemy appeared, to them, invariably to quit their guns; and ... threw themselves prostrate on the decks, to escape, if possible, the effects of the discharge.'[87]

This must not be taken to diminish in any way either the heroic efforts of both officers and men on the British side or Nelson's own contribution to Sir John Jervis' fleet's success. *Captain*, for example, consumed 146 barrels of gunpowder that day, and used up all her 64-pounder carronade balls and grape-shot. The resourceful gun-crews therefore loaded each of their carronades with seven 9-pounder balls, the effect of which at close range must have been, if anything, even more frightful. Nor should it be supposed that the Spaniards were all lacking in courage; on the four ships captured, 20 – 25 per cent of their crews were lost before they surrendered.[88]

Maybe it was their traditional reticence that prevented contemporary

---

87 The British response, as a broadside was about to be received, was to repeat the before-dinner grace 'For what we are about to receive...'

88 Article by Colin White in 'Battle of Cape St Vincent' Bicentennial Conference notes.

Englishmen from describing the full reality of the horrors of war, and especially of being on the losing side. Such reticence did not prevent two midshipmen on the USS *Constitution* reporting what it was like to go on board the British frigate HMS *Guerriere* (38) and HMS *Levant* (an 18 gun corvette) after they had been taken by the *Constitution*[89] in the War of 1812. On *Guerriere* Henry Gilliam found the decks with

> 'pieces of skulls, brains, legs, arms & blood ... in every directions [sic] and groanes [sic] of the wounded were almost enough to make me curse the war.'

On going over with the Third Lieutenant to accept *Levant*'s surrender, another midshipman described how he found her quarter-deck;

> 'The mizen [sic] mast for several feet was covered with brains and blood; teeth, pieces of bones, fingers and large pieces of flesh were picked up from off the deck. It was a long time before I could familiarize myself to these...'

A British account of the gory reality of war is to be found in a letter[90] after Trafalgar from George Castle, a midshipman on *Royal Sovereign* (Collingwood's flagship) to his sister;

> '...I looked once out of our stern ports – but saw nothing but French and Spaniards round firing at us in all directions – it was shocking to see many brave seamen mangled so, some with their heads half shot away, other[s] with their entrails mashed lying panting on the deck, the greatest slaughter was on the quarter deck and Poop...'

That night the British fleet again kept close order, with *Niger* out to windward as lookout to keep an eye on the Spanish fleet. Only four ships had been taken, and there was a real danger that, next day, they would renew the battle and, with their superior numbers, reverse the St. Valentine's Day decision.

The huge four-decker *Santissima Trinidad* (the largest battle ship in the world) had been crippled in her fight with Nelson's *Captain* and had lost all three masts. She was last seen being towed back towards Cadiz by a Spanish frigate. Jervis ordered *Minerve* to search for her. On 17 February she was joined by the frigate *Emerald* whose captain, Berkeley, was senior to Cockburn and had come with orders to take command of a squadron consisting of *Niger, la Minerve*, his own ship and a sloop.

---

[89] She was nominally a frigate but carried 54 guns (mostly 24-pounders), displaced some 2,000 tons (as against about 1,100 tons for *la Minerve*) and was over 200 ft long. Her hard-fought victories over these British ships, and her equally bloody capture and sinking of HMS *Java* (which happened to be carrying the plans for HMS *Tricomalee* to India, where she was to be built) were hardly surprising.

[90] First published in *The Times*, 21 October 1912 and reproduced in the Nelson Dispatch, October 1998.

After three days they found *Santissima Trinidad* some 80 miles south-east of Cape St Vincent, still under tow but by now having jury masts and sails rigged. The log reads;

> 'Tuesday February 21st 1797. Fresh Gales. At 3 saw two strange Sails to ENE; at ¾ past 4 wore ship answered sig'l to prepare for battle, and found the Chase to be a Spanish four deck ship and a Frigate. The Spanish Frigate set her Courses and Topsls. At 6 wore ship, the Spanish ship 3 miles… *Emerald* and Squad.n in Company. Join'd H.M.Ship *Terpsicore*…'

Minerve, being faster than the others, got there first. Rather than defend her charge, the escorting Spanish frigate cast off her tow and escaped. There were plenty of precedents for two or more frigates to take on, and beat, a single 'ship of the line', including the loss of the damaged *Berwick*, with Samuel on board, to three French frigates in 1795. The four-decker ship's guns were, of course, still fully operative, even if she could not be sailed properly, so Cockburn approached from dead astern of her and, when right up behind her, 'wore ship'[91] and luffed up to bring *Minerve* up under her stern. There her enormous main armament could not reach him with their devastating broadsides, even though her 'stern chasers' were firing.

His intention was to deliver a broadside with his own not inconsiderable main guns. He would fire a 'raking shot' right through her stern windows and down her gun decks, where frightful carnage would have ensued, his guns double-shotted with both grape and ball, just as Nelson had done with *Ça Ira* two years before. Down below on the gun deck the guns were ready loaded, run out and aimed. The firing lanyards were in the gun captains' hands ready to fire the moment the order was given. Cockburn was on the very point of opening fire. But at that precise moment the unbelievable happened. To his utter astonishment, and to the disbelief of the gun-crews, Berkeley signalled *Minerve* to return to *Emerald*. This he did. In the approaching dusk, *Santissima Trinidad* disappeared.

It is hard to understand why Cockburn, cast in Nelson's mould and well known for his dash and daring, did not at least fire one broadside before turning away, even if he did not actually feel able to 'turn a blind eye' and ignore the order.

According to one account, she was not found again. 'Clowes', however,

---

[91] i.e. he went about by bringing *Minerve*'s stern through the wind rather than her bows. This could take longer than 'tacking' but meant, in effect, turning in her own length – safer with 130 guns trying to bear on him! It also meant that she could be brought about onto the other tack without taking men away from the guns.

maintains that shortly after 6pm another frigate not under Berkeley's command, *Terpsichore*, 32 guns, under Captain Richard Bowen, came up, but did not follow Berkeley who was by then sailing away northwards. He soon parted company and carried on alone. He found *Santissima Trinidad* at 7pm on 28 February and engaged her the following day, again on his own, but he was not able to make any impression so he kept shadowing her until, off Cape Spartel, she joined other ships of the Spanish fleet. Next morning the *Minerve* took the brig which had been accompanying the *Santisima Trinidad.*

Berkeley's decision deprived Samuel of the honour of taking part in a single ship action that would have gone down in history as 'David versus Goliath', a single frigate taking or destroying the biggest 'ship of the line' in the world. He would probably also have gained a fourth clasp to his medal and, perhaps more important to him, a share of the resulting prize money and head money.

Inevitably, there was a demand for a court martial. The charge against Berkeley, and brought against him by his own officers, was that he had been quite wrong to call off *Minerve* at the very point of opening fire. His defence was that an unidentified ship had been seen bearing down on them. She was coming from the direction of Cadiz. He therefore assumed her to be the enemy, even though she later turned out to be a British ship.

Cockburn could have been vindictive in his evidence had he wished. He said he was sorry not to have been able to pit his cockleshell against the 134 massive guns of the *Santissima Trinidad,* but he did not know what state she was in. So far as he could see, she was quite capable of seeing off any number of British frigates; even though the heavy sea meant that she could not open her lower gun ports, she still had three more decks of guns. In his hurry to get under her stern he had half filled *Minerve's* main deck with water, and he believed *Emerald* to be in the same condition. *Niger* was, by then, nowhere near and there was every possibility of the Spanish frigate having a change of heart and re-entering the fray. On this evidence, the court martial was stopped.

CHAPTER 6

Nelson had for long been thinking of a raid on Santa Cruz on the island of Tenerife, in the Canary Islands, but knew that it needed the help of the army. He had in mind the 3,700 soldiers taken off Elba, but the army refused to co-operate, not being dazzled by the thought of the Spanish treasure ships rumoured to be on their way as Nelson evidently was. He might well have let it rest there, but for the exploits of *Minerve* and *Lively*.

After the Battle of Cape St Vincent, the British fleet put into Lagos to lick its wounds and refit. *Minerve* was sent close inshore to see what was going on at Cadiz and reported back that a huge fleet, including 25 ships of the line and ten frigates, was there. Jervis (his Earldom had not yet come through) wrote to Cockburn;

> '*Victory* off Cape Roxent
> 26th of February1797.
>
> Dear Sir
> Should this letter reach you, you are hereby authorised, to remain cruizing for one month from this date, between Cape St. Vincent, & Cape Spartel.
> I am Sir
> your very humble Servant
> J JERVIS
>
> Captain Cockburn,
> His Majesty's Ship *La Minerve*.'

As Nelson's ship *Captain* was still out of action, he was next sent on a cruise in *Irresistible* with *Zealous* and *Culloden*, accompanied by *la Minerve*, with orders to look out for the Viceroy of Mexico. He wrote;

> *Irresistable*, off Lagos Bay, March 16th, 1797.
> 'I am here looking for the Viceroy of Mexico, with three Sail of the Line, and hope to meet him. Two First rates and a 74 are with him; but the larger the ships the better the mark, and who will not fight for dollars?'[92]

These instructions must have gladdened the hearts of 'the Minerves', as her crew called themselves, and all on board the three ships-of-the-line with her. It was

---

[92] Letter 16 March 1797 to Adml Hood's secretary, John M'Arthur, who was one of Nelson's prize agents.

said that the Viceroy was due in Cadiz from Havana any day now, accompanied by an equal force of ships; in other words, a 'walkover' to a British squadron, who felt confident of taking on, and beating, any force of up to 50 per cent. greater firepower. More important by far to the officers and men alike, however, was the cargo he was bringing with him; not just a small quantity of gold, but it was said to be worth six or even seven million pounds! With such a vast prize in the offing (quite apart from the value of the three ships carrying it) even the common seaman's tiny share of the anticipated prize money must have driven them all nearly crazy with anticipation.

So for the two months following the Battle of Cape St Vincent, *Minerve* patrolled between the north west tip of Africa and Cape St Vincent, looking for the fleet of Spanish treasure ships which Nelson confidently expected to be there. But, alas, the search was not successful. Rations were short, scurvy was rife on board (two men died from it) and morale rapidly fell to a very low level.

On rejoining the fleet, Cockburn was told by Nelson of his plans for a raid on Santa Cruz. Whilst Earl St Vincent remained on blockade duty off Cadiz, trying to bring the Spanish fleet out to battle, and Nelson's squadron went to Elba, *Minerve* and *Lively* (which had rejoined the fleet after hurrying home to England with the news of the victory in February) would be sent to mount a raid on Santa Cruz. Captain Hallowell, *Lively's* captain, was 12 years Cockburn's senior and was therefore to be in overall command.

Quickly replenishing her stores (including lemons to counteract the outbreak of scurvy) *Minerve* rejoined the fleet for a further fortnight's blockade duty off Cadiz and then, at the end of April 1797, the two frigates headed for Tenerife, 1,000 miles south.

The Canaries are a group of islands some 300 miles long. The two ships did not pass too close to Santa Cruz in order not to arouse suspicion but, instead, cruised along the islands to see what they could find. Richard Cambridge, a member of what is now the Dorset regiment, a detachment of which were on board *Minerve* instead of Marines, whose punishments feature so often in the log book, was given four dozen lashes for neglect and disobedience.

On 27 May they looked in at Santa Cruz in the early morning and *Lively* sent a boat in, under a flag of truce, with a letter for the governor about a suggested exchange of prisoners. Rightly suspecting a ruse, and that the real intention was to examine the harbour and the shipping there, the governor sent out a launch to meet them before they came in too close. According to the official Spanish account of the incident[93] the ruse was about as thin as could be. They suggested an exchange of prisoners but, as they were forced to admit that they had no Spaniards, but only French prisoners, the Governor said he was not interested. Nevertheless, they saw a massive treasure ship lying under the security of the guns in the fortress and also what looked like a French brig; her nationality was amply confirmed when they were loudly abused in French by her crew for coming too close.

Hallowell and Cockburn decided that it would not be possible for the frigates themselves to 'cut out' the two ships in so strongly defended a harbour. Instead, a 'boat action' would be organised under Hardy[94] whose privilege it was, as senior first lieutenant, to lead it. Two days later the two frigates returned. It is interesting to compare the two versions of the Captain's Journal. First, the version at the Public Record Office at Kew;

> 'Moderate breezes with thick hazy weather... At 12 past 10 hove to, hoisted boats out. At 11 sent the boats in company with the *Lively's*, manned and armed into the Bay to cut out a French man-of-war brig at an anchorage there. At ½ past 3 they began to fire from the shore at our boats; our large cutter received so many shot that she sank and was lost. At 6 the boats returned with the brig in tow. She proved to be *La Mutine* from Brest ... mounting 12 six-pounders and two 42-pound carronades and 140 men. At 8 filled and made sail with the *Lively* and brig in company. Received on board 42 prisoners.'

Next, Cockburn's copy;[95]

> 'Saturday May 27th 1797 ... *Lively* in Co, the People emp'd Working up Junk and rigging a spare foretopsl yard...
>
> 'Sunday May 28th 1797. Mustered Ship's Comp[y]. by Divisions
>
> 'Monday May 29th 1797. *Lively* in Comp[y]. People emp'd clearing away the Boats. LYING TO [sic] OFF THE TOWN OF SANTA CRUZ. At 12 past 10 hove to, hoisting Boats out, at 11 sent the Boats in comp[y] with the *Lively* man'd and arm'd into the Bay. Took out a French Man of War Brig ... at 6 the Boats returned with the Brig in tow...'

Hallowell's report to the Secretary to the Lords Commissioners of the Admiralty in the London Gazette, as reprinted in the Gentleman's Magazine, gives only slightly more detail;

---

93 Piraterias y Ataques Navales contra las Islas' Canarias [Madrid, 1950].
94 Thomas Masterman Hardy, Victory's captain at Trafalgar.
95 On microfilm at the National Maritime Museum Library at Greenwich and the Portsmouth Central Library.

'To Evan Nepean Eſq.

Lively, S.W. End of Teneriffe, May 31.

Sir, I have the honour to inform you, that on ſtanding into the Bay of Santa Cruz, in the iſland of Teneriffe, on the afternoon of the 28th, in company with *La Minerve*, I diſcovered an armed brig lying in the road, which, on our nearer approach, hoiſted French colours. Capt. Cockburn agreeing with myſelf in opinion that ſhe might be taken from her anchors, I ordered all boats of the two ſhips, with a Lieutenant in each, the next night to bring her out. Lieut. Hardy, of *La Minerve*, being the ſenior officer, the command fell on him. At about half-paſt two in the afternoon, he made a most reſolute attack, in which he was gallantly ſupported by Lieutenants Bland, Hopkins, and Buſhby, and Lieut. Bulkeley, of the marines, in the *Lively's* boats, and Lieutenants Gage and Marling in *la Minerve's* boats, and, under a ſmart fire of muſquetry from the brig, boarded and carried her almoſt immediately. This gave an alarm to the town, and a heavy fire of artillery and muſquetry was opened from every part of the garriſon, and from a large ſhip lying there in the road immediately, which continued without intermiſſion for nearly an hour, during which time they were very much expoſed in getting the brig under weigh, and towing her out, there being very little wind, and a little before 4 o'clock they had got out of reach of the batteries with *La Mutine* French national corvette, of 12 6-pounders, and 2 36-pounder carronades, and 135 men, 113 of whom were on-board at the time, commanded by Citizen Xavier Panmier, Capitain de Fregate. She ſailed from Breſt on the 8th ... and had put into the Bay of Santa Cruz three days before ſhe was captured, to take in water. The captain was on ſhore at the time. Lieut. Hardy having command of the boats on this expedition, I have ſent him in with the prize, and cannot recommend him, or the officers or ſeaman employed on that ſervice with him, in too ſtrong terms. Incloſed is a liſt of the wounded[96] belonging to both ſhips.

BENJ. HALLOWELL.'

The two accounts differ as to times and in other details, but it seems clear that the boat attack went in during broad daylight. A 'cutting out' expedition would normally be expected to take place during the hours of darkness, preferably when there was no moon. So why was this one launched in broad daylight – at two-thirty in the afternoon?

The answer is simple. The Spaniards were no fools. They knew two of His Britannic Majesty's war ships had called the previous day, and were bound to be

---

96   15 of Lieutenant Hardy's party, including himself and a midshipman, were wounded, but none killed.

still in the vicinity. The British had managed to spy out the harbour. They would most likely have known of Hallowell's and Cockburn's reputations (they were both, under Nelson, known for their enterprise, dash and daring) and they probably considered it to be at least even money that they would shortly call again, almost certainly at night. That night had been spent at arms, a sleepless night. So Hallowell realised that he could, indeed, achieve the vital element of surprise after all – by sending Hardy in with the ships' boats that day, during siesta time!

This was the 'Boat Action' for which Samuel Blackmore was later awarded the third and final clasp to his Naval General Service medal. It was probably an event that the men wished to celebrate. The unfortunate soldier Richard Cambridge, no doubt also celebrating the successful outcome, yet again received three dozen lashes, this time for theft and drunkenness. It may have been no coincidence that part of the cargo from the prize *la Mutine* transferred to *Minerve*, where it could be guarded more effectively by an armed marine guard, included a large quantity of brandy;

> 'The People empd. hoisting in provisions from the Prize ... rec'd the follow-
> ing provisions, viz ... 10 Galls Brandy.'

They also helped themselves to as many of *Mutine's* stores as they could, including copper sheets, rope and carpenter's stores, and two 36-pounder carronades – these may have been the 42-pounders mentioned above.

Then, as now, everyone had to 'cover himself' by putting everything into writing, even in such a small ship, and even when they were engaged on such a mission; a letter in the Cockburn papers in the Library at the National Maritime Museum at Greenwich reads;

'La Minerve in the Tagus
April 27th 1797

Sir

  The Neceſsaries supplied for the use of the Sick, & hurt Seamen, and Marines, on board His Majesty's Ship *La Minerve* under your Command, being all Expended, & the time for which they were to serve, having elapsed the 12th of April last

  I have to request, you will be pleased to order a supply of Neceſsaries, for Six Months, for her complement of 300 Men.

    I am Sir
    your most Oblgd. & Humble Servt.
       JACOB MOUNTGARRET
       Surgeon

To

George Cockburn Esq.

Captain of His Majesty's Ship

La Minerve.'

Another letter, similarly addressed, was possibly intended to put the captain on the spot in case there was a further outbreak of scurvy;

La Minerve June 27th

1797 Funchall

Sir

I have to request you will please to give me an Order, to purchase onions, & Fruits for the use of the Sick, & hurt Seamen & Marines, on board His Majesty's Ship *La Minerve* under your Command, for her complement of 300 men.

I have the Honor [sic] to be

Sir

your most Oblgd. & Hmbl. Servt.

JACOB MOUNTGARRET'

When the transfer of stores was completed, *la Mutine* was sent back to rejoin Nelson with a prize crew under Hardy. Samuel was, according to the muster book, not one of those 'lent' to her, but remained on *Minerve*. Two days later, *Minerve* lost her main and mizzen topmasts and her fore topgallant mast in a squall. She was being hard pressed. It was decided she could no longer carry her prisoners so, back at Santa Cruz, she put them on shore under another flag of truce, before carrying on cruising round the Canaries. At the end of June they returned 300 miles north to Funchal, on Madeira, to re-provision, taking on board plenty of fresh beef and wine and, more important, 170 hanks of onions to combat the continuing attack of scurvy.

A certain amount of shore leave was granted, but some of the men failed to return to their ship on time, and there was much grumbling. Cockburn was worried that the 'Great Mutinies' at home could break out in the Mediterranean Fleet. News of the mutinies had certainly already reached the men who could not but sympathise with most of the complaints that gave rise to them.

All hands were yet again mustered aft to witness punishment; a man was given three dozen lashes for inciting mutiny and discharged from the ship. They were mustered aft again on 19 June when a man was punished for quarrelling and treating an officer with disrespect. The ship's company were mustered by divisions for prayers on Sunday 25 June, and again the Articles of War were read to them. But there was yet again a call for all hands to muster aft on the following Tuesday. The captain's log clearly gives the impression that the crew's morale was at an all-time low;

> 'Set up the main rigging: punish'd James Furguson with 2 doz & 8 lashes for Mutinous Language & breaking his leave on Shore; also Jno. Lee for breaking his leave with 1 doz lashes ... the People Emp'd Watering & getting ready for sea.'

The log does not explain what had led to this. The arrival the previous day of a convoy from England, bound for the West Indies, was viewed with apprehension when it was found that one of the escorts, the frigate *Thames*, was badly infected by the Nore and Spithead mutinies. Cockburn wrote to his friend Nelson a month later explaining what had happened;

> 'I had heard before your letter arrived too much concerning the mutiny at home by the arrival ... of the *Thames* who was in such a state as I suppose no ship ever was before ... the men doing exactly what they pleased and the officers being absolutely afraid to control them. They endeavoured to persuade our men to act like themselves, telling them they turned all the officers they disliked out of the ships and that they did exactly what they pleased in the Channel ships and they even threatened if our people did not mutiny to write against them to the seamen in England; and on being refused leave to come on board of us, swam under the bows to bring inflammatory papers, which were given up by our people. Indeed, I had every reason to be very much pleased with the conduct of the majority of our ship's company (in the midst of temptation) who, on my turning them up [i.e. having them all mustered aft] on account of some suspicion about them, assured me of their firm attachment to their government and officers and offered to prove it by going alongside either of the other frigates that should behave improperly. In spite of this, however, since we have been out I have been informed that some few of them had been tainted by the *Thames*, but finding the generality of their shipmates against them they kept silent.'

Captain Hallowell in *Lively* was not so fortunate. Cockburn's enlightened policy of allowing shore leave whenever possible had no small part to play here, as *Minerve's* men had already had shore leave before *Thames* arrived, and were back on board again. But *Lively* arrived after her. Hallowell was not happy at the idea of his men being on shore at the same time as men from *Thames*, so he allowed alcohol to be consumed on board instead which, under the circumstances, was hardly a wise decision. Cockburn's letter to Nelson continues;

> 'The *Lively* ... broke out ... by giving three cheers but they were almost instantly quelled and....most of their ringleaders were most severely flogged and one of them is in irons to be tried by court martial.'

The three captains held an investigation on board the *Thames*;

> '...where things came out that Captain Lukin had not an idea of. It seemed that six or eight of his people had the rest completely under subjection, that they could do with the ship whatever they pleased; and one of these men had said ... he did not know if he would permit her to go to the West Indies, but if he did it would be only to make the fleet there mutiny...'

The trouble makers were taken out of *Thames* and sent for Court Martial, Cockburn adding in his letter to Nelson;

> '...I hope they will have a different part to act in the West Indies to what they expected.'

Minerve and *Lively* then returned to the Canaries and had a busy month capturing prizes – a sure cure for low morale. One of them, with a prize crew of only an officer and eight men from *Minerve*, herself took a further prize. With so many prizes they returned to Funchal to drop them off, then back to the Canaries again.

On 1 September they chased a ship during the night and found her to be a French ship, the *Marseillais* [sic], 28 guns. She ran for shelter and put into the harbour at Gran Canary Island which was defended by two strong shore batteries. *Minerve* cheekily followed her in (relying on the pilot on board *Marseillais* to guide her in, too!) and came along-side her. In spite of continuous fire from the shore batteries she overcame her before daybreak and managed to sail her out of the harbour. There was but the lightest of winds and they were only just off a lee shore. Again, *Minerve's* log tells us the story in masterly brevity; it seems to have been written by a lieutenant who was more concerned at the possibility of having the cost of the missing equipment deducted from his meagre pay than recording a triumph of British naval history!

> 'At 2 chase hoisted French colours; fired several shots at her to bring her to. At 4 chase standing into Porto Confital Bay. Half past 4 chase anchored between the two batteries and opened a heavy fire on us, as did the two batteries. Anchored with a spring on the best bower in 10 fathoms; hove in on the spring[97] and brought our broadside to bear on the batteries and ship, and then engaged them. At 5 the ship struck. Sent an officer onboard to take possession of her. She proved to be the *Marseillais*... At 10 minutes before 6, hove short but not being able to purchase the anchor, it having hooked a

---

[97] A 'spring' was a line with one end tied to the stern of the ship and the other to the anchor cable near to but ahead of the ship. At anchor, a ship would lie facing the tide or the wind (depending on their relative strengths) but, with a spring, she could be pulled right round across the wind or tide until her guns squarely faced the desired target.

rock, and the forts keeping up a heavy fire on us, cut the cable by order of the Captain. Lost the anchor and 12 fathoms of cable, and the spring which was a six and a half inch hawser, and which was 96 fathom. Made all sail with the boats ahead at 7. Light airs with a heavy swell setting on the land. At 8 prize in company. At 2pm finding the ship drifting fast ashore, let go the small bower in 30 fathoms about 2 cables from the surf. Carried the stream anchor out with the stream cable, a 9 inch cablet and a 7½ inch hawser bent to it. At 3 carried the keg [i.e. the kedge anchor] with 138 fathom of cablet bent to it. At 5 a breeze sprang up; set all sail, ran the ship ahead by the hawsers and then cut the small bower cable and hawsers, and cleared the outer rock by about ½ cable's length.'

Cockburn wrote to the French Consul at Santa Cruz about some prisoners, and also wrote to the Spanish Governor;

'La Minerve off Teneriffe

11th September 1797

Sir

I had the honor to write your Excellency on the 5th Inst, acquainting you that I had been obliged, owing to the Ship not being able to work up to the Town, to land 28 Spanish, & 23 French prisoners (at their own request) on the western end of the Island of Teneriffe, & requesting you would have the goodnefs to send me the receipts for them, & in return, any Englishmen that might be on the Island.

I now therefore send His Majesty's Sloop El Corso, to receive the said receipts, & Englishmen, being convinced from your Excellency's former conduct, that you will not hesitate to send them.

I feel it necefsary to aquaint you, that the Flag of truce I sent with the above mentioned Prisoners, was very improperly treated, & the Officers that commanded the Boats were taken by an armed Mob, & detained a whole day without any victuals.

As I am convinced this could not be with the sanction of your Excellency, I shall take no further notice of it, but trust you will give such directions, as will in future protect our Boats from similar instances of inconvenience, & Insult.

I have the Honor to be
With great consideration
Your Excellency's Obdt. Servt.
G. COCKBURN.

To
His Excellency the
Governor of Teneriffe
Santa Cruz.'

After dropping off her prisoners at the western end of Tenerife, *Minerve* put into Funchal again to re-provision and continued north with her prizes to rejoin the fleet off Cadiz, the log recording;

> 'In hoisting in the jolly boat, the tackle fall gave way and John Slade, seaman, fell out of her and was drowned; although we lowered the cutter immediately, yet was too late to save him.'

Detailed eye-witness accounts of these particular 'Boat Service' and 'cutting out' actions have not been traced, but Jacob Nagle's Journal gives accounts of similar events. 'Cutting out' operations, as any reader of the 'Hornblower' novels by C.S. Forester[98] will know, were normally carried out with muffled oars at dead of night when there was no moon. Men, armed to the teeth, their faces darkened with charcoal or soot, would quietly row alongside their unsuspecting target, climb silently up the anchor cable, slit the sentry's throat and throw down below anyone who offered resistance. Then they would hoist sail, cut the anchor cable and sail her out to sea.

Here is an example of a cutting-out raid by *Blanche* and her crew, intended to capture two brigs and a gun-boat, that went wrong. It also shows what it was like to receive red-hot cannon balls[99] from shore-based guns specially equipped to heat them up in order to cause fires on board. This is a problem *Minerve* would inevitably have encountered at Santa Cruz, assuming that the Spaniards manning the forts had time to get their stock of cannon balls red-hot. The unique spelling is Nagle's;

> 'Purceiving two brigs and a gun boat laying in a small bay abreast of a small village under cover of a tower that mounted eight thirty-two pounders completed for firing hot shot, about a leven o'clock Nelson made a signal to enter the bay. We ketching a light breeze of wind, we ran in within musket shot of the shore, but the wind dying away and fell dead calm, we lay like a target under their guns, both great guns and small arms, and Nelson and the squadron could not get in to our assistance. The shot from the tower being hot shot, therefore, one watch was employed with fierbuckets and the other half at their quarters. We receiv'd one shot abreast the fore magizene and set us afier, but supplying it well with water till we could clear away below and cut it out, as fortune favoured us the shot was two large to fall between the lineing and the ships out side plank. If it had been smaller it would of fell

---

98 Forester, as well as writing the 'Hornblower' series, also wrote serious books on naval history.
99 Later in his career, Cockburn was bombarding a fort that was raining red hot shot down on his ship. He managed to get one lucky shot in through a gun embrasure and hit the furnace. It blew up, with the result that the whole fort was burned down.

down under the magizeine where we could not get at it and would of blown the ship up....Another shot struck us on the quarter and set us on fire, entering the gunroom....

'Captain Sawyer made a signal to Com'd. Nelson to purmit us to engage, but he anull'd the signal which was lucky for us. If we had been engaging, what with the fire and smoke, we should of not seen where we ware on fier until it would of been two late to put it out. I was stationed as capt of the 5 guns from forward... A hot shot entered the chestree and passed the back of my neck. Having tied hair, it cut and singed my hair without doing any more damage to me... The officer of the deck coming along at that moment ordered me to lay down, and ... the shot entered which would of beheaded me completely. The same shot ... kill'd some fowls in the hen coobs a midships...

'All this time we had sent our boats to bring the brigs off and the gun boat. The men had left them, but they were hard and fast ashore and a continued fire upon them with musketry from the shore, and having several wounded, we left them. After laying in this situation for the space of three hours and no breeze springing up, Nelson made the signal for all boats from the squodron. They came in and took us in toe, they quit firing upon us and began firing at the boats, but it was in vain, the boats being low in the water and in constant motion. They took us out without loss of a man'.

Nagle gives an account of another cutting-out expedition which also proved to be abortive;

'Some time after, running off Vardo, we discovered a French sloop of war mored close to the shore and gunboats laying round hur under the heavy fort over hur mast heads. As soon as dark came on, Nelson ordered eight boats from different ships with two marines in each boat, besides the boats crews, armed, and an officer, his first lieutenant, commander. We pulled into the eastermost part of the bay and pulled a long shore, one boats painter fast to the other in a line, with our oars muffled til we got within about 15 yards of the vessel, when a gunboat that lay within us let fly an 18 pounder shot over the center of us. The sentry on bd the brig was so much fritened that he could not utter himself when he attempted to hail us. If the gunboat had not kept a better lookout than the brig, we would of been on board in less than three minutes, but being discover'd, the commanding officers orders was to cast loose and run. Our leut. was for boarding, but it was two late. We pulled out for the offin. The batteries on the mount opened upon us with grape and canister, and dropped round us like hail, but as God would have it a dark cloud came over the mount [?moon] that moment which compel'd them to fier at random. It was surprising how we could escape without a man being hurt....We returned on board.'

A happier account is given by Jacob Nagle of an expedition that succeeded. Again, the spelling is Nagle's;

> 'Beside the squadron we had two gunboats that was taken by the squadron... Those two sneaked a long shore in the day time, to give us information. Then at night Nelson would send in boats to cut them out.

> 'At this time the French had command all a long the coast. Coming of Ville Frank we stood off from land till night, then stood in and hoisted out two boats from each ship and went in with muffled oars... We then pulled a long shore under the forts, so close that we could of fired at the sentries with our pistols. They having fiers and lanthorns and we being in the dark, they could not purceive us... We then passed the town and took a cirkle round the bay. We then spied some boats. We made for them and boarded with cutlashes, making such a clattering with the weapons they cried out for quarters, expecting death at any moment, but they proved to be poor fishermen. We went on and left them.

> 'The next we spied a ship. We came up with hur and boarded hur in three divisions. She was full of men. They were resolute though they had no arms... She proved to be a French ship full of Austrons, prisoners to the French, but when they found we ware English they did rejoice, and afterwards a great number entered on board of Nelsons ship.

> 'By this time daylight was apearing, and it came on to blow a smart gale ... but we could sea no ships. We up hellem and put the boats before the wind ... being a heavy following sea and the boat very low, it took 3 and 4 hand abailing the water out. In about one hour we ... discovered our own frigate about three leagues ahead of us ... and in a short time we came a long side with the boat half full of water. We hoisted the boat in and we ware order'd to our hammoks after we had some refreshment.'

The only time that *Minerve* and *Blanche* were together was during the six months run-up to the *Sabina* affair and at Elba afterwards. But for every action involving *Blanche* that did not involve *Minerve* there was at least one where *Minerve* was involved and *Blanche* was not, so no apology is made for boring the reader by quoting so much from the Nagle Journal. He paints a picture that would not have been in the least unfamiliar to Samuel Blackmore.

On hearing of Hardy's feat in taking the *Mutine* at Santa Cruz, Earl St Vincent promptly promoted him commander in charge of *la Mutine* – his first independent command. St Vincent subsequently wrote to Nelson;

> 'My dear Admiral. The capture of *la Mutine* was so desperate an enterprise, that I should certainly have promoted Lieutenant Hardy, so that neither you, Hallowell, nor Cockburn, have any debtor account to me upon this occa-

sion. He has got it by his own bat, and I hope will prosper'.

By the time officialdom got round to issuing the 1793-1840 Naval General Service medal in 1848, very few (particularly of those involved in the earlier actions) survived to claim them. Only four, Samuel and three others (Cockburn being one of them[100]) claimed for *la Minerve's* action with *Sabina* in December 1796. Only Samuel and two others (one of them Cockburn) claimed for the 'Boat Service' at Santa Cruz in May 1797, and there were, in all, only 364 claimants for Cape St Vincent in February 1797.[101] The highest number of clasps awarded to any one man was seven; Cockburn and four others were awarded six. The grant of the medal was announced in the London gazette in these terms;

'ADMIRALTY, 1st June, 1847

> Her Majesty having been graciously pleased to command that a medal should be struck to record the services of her Fleets and Armies during the war commencing in 1793... All officers, Petty officers, Seamen and Marines, who consider that they are entitled to receive this mark of their Sovereign's gracious recollection of their services, and of Her desire to record the same ... are to send, in writing, the statement of their claims ... specifying for what action, and at what period of time, the claim is preferred...'[102]

A book on medals says that NGS medals with 'Boat Service' clasps are not as popular with collectors as those for Trafalgar, for example, but appeal to collectors with naval interests; they were well earned, as such expeditions carried no passengers. The medal bears a portrait of the 'young' queen on the front (obverse) and Britannia riding a sea horse on the reverse. It is carried on a white ribbon with dark blue edges, and a silver clasp on the ribbon marks each action for which it was awarded. The sailor's name is engraved round the edge of the rim, but not the name of his ship.

Arriving off Cadiz on 14 October 1797, *Minerve* was ordered by St Vincent to go to Gibraltar for repairs, and to leave her prizes there. Ever mindful of his crew's needs, Cockburn obviously had the same feeling for the soldiers on his ship who were serving as marines, for on arriving at Gibraltar he wrote;

---

[100] By then 'The Right Honourable Sir George Cockburn, PC, GCB, FRS, MP, Admiral of the Red'.

[101] Hardy died in 1839 so he never got his medal. A most hideous memorial to him, in the form of what looks like a Victorian mill chimney 72 ft high, was erected where he lived at Portesham, near Abbotsbury, in Dorset.

[102] 'Nelson Commemorative Medals 1797-1905' by Thomas A Hardy (The Nelson Society 1985).

'La Minerve Gibraltar Oct 28th 1797

Sir

A Detachment of the 11th Regt. doing duty as Marines on board His Majesty's *La Minerve* under my Command, being very much in want of Cloathing, none of them having received any since the 5th of July 1794, & there being no Officer of the Regiment here to obtain any for them, I have thought it right to represent their situation to you, & to request you will give such directions herein as may appear to you proper.

I have the Honor to be
Sir
Your Obedt. humble Servant
G. COCKBURN.

to Lieut Genl. O'Hara
etc.. etc.. etc.
Gibraltar'

With his ship lying alongside the mole and 'stripped' whilst the dockyard men swarmed all over her, her powder removed for safety's sake, Cockburn found himself Senior Naval Officer there. He took command of three small oared gunboats which he manned with some of *Minerve's* crew and, with them, routed thirty similar Spanish gunboats which were about to attack a British convoy that had become becalmed. The fight continued for four hours, in the dark. Only one ship of the convoy, an army victualler, was lost. Her master had been killed and most of her crew had abandoned her. Cockburn's report to Earl St Vincent said;

'I put some hands on board of her to endeavour to get her sails set again, but we found everything cut to pieces by the shot. I therefore took her in tow but the wind unfortunately springing up ... I could not keep her off; I kept her in tow however, a considerable time in the hopes of a change, till she drifted so close to Algeciras, when seeing no possible chance of getting her off, and all the rest of the convoy having got clear, and being myself nearly surrounded by the enemy's gunboats, I thought proper after withdrawing my people from her, to make my way after the rest of the convoy, all of which safely anchored here by half past 4 o'clock.'

Other duties as Senior Naval Officer were less exacting; a letter in Cockburn's papers at the National Library of Congress reads;

'Gibraltar new Mole 6th Nov 1797

Sir

Having been superseded by Thos. Stepthenson Esq. in the Command of His Majesty's Bomb *Thunder* – I am therefore to request you will please to order a Survey to be held on her remains of Boatswains Stores, for the purpose of delivering them into the charge of her present Commander, there being no Boatswain appointed.

I am Sir

your most obdet. Servt.

L.BLAND

To
George Cockburn Esq.
Captain of His Majesty's Ship *La Minerve*
    &
Senior Officer at Gibraltar.'

Minerve was ready for sea again on 25 November. She was ordered back to the Atlantic, to meet up again with Ben Hallowell, who was now in command of *Swiftsure* (74), south of Madeira. The ship's company were glad to hear the captain's orders;

> 'You are to cruise in the best possible position for capturing the enemy's privateers which infest those seas, and interrupting the trade to and from Spain and her colonies until January 10, 1798, when you are to make the best of your way back to the Tagus.'

It took more than a week to find Hallowell, so Cockburn interpreted his orders as meaning that he should extend his cruise accordingly. On 18 January *Minerve* took three prizes (although none of them very large) in one day. Dropping these off in Gibraltar, Cockburn returned to the Tagus.

Hardy's Monument, near Abbotsbury, Dorset.

CHAPTER 7

Meanwhile, back at Cadiz, the blockade had continued in *la Minerve's* absence. The Spanish convoy was still eagerly anticipated on both sides. The population flocked to the city walls every morning to see if it had arrived, and they petitioned their Admiralty to order their fleet out to drive the British away, fearing the convoy may already have fallen into their hands. But what was left of the Spanish fleet remained in the safety of the harbour and rightly declined to come out and risk a further defeat.

Blockade duty, although highly necessary, was also highly unpleasant, particularly during winter Atlantic gales. It was also mind-numbingly boring. *Minerve* and her crew had more than their fair share of it. More ships were lost to the weather than to the enemy. Less than half of the crew were actually needed[103] to sail the ship and man the sails; the full complement were only needed to man the guns, without which a war ship would have had no meaning. Scrubbing the decks and the daily gunnery practice were as much to keep the crew occupied as anything else. Jacob Nagle in *Blanche* was outside Cadiz for a whole year, and yet in his 'Journal', written many years later, he said it was only a month;

> 'In a few days [6 June 1797] we joined Jarvises fleet off Cadis. Jarvises fleet lay at anchor out side, then Nelson with a squadron of seven sail of the line lay inside of them, and we were stationed within the whole, laying off and on from one shore to the other, all hands at quarters during the night with the hatches laid over that no one was allowed to go below, and let us stand on the one tack or the other, we would have a shot or a shell flying over us during the night. The reason was to keep the gun boats off from anoying the line of battle ships. The gunboats would come and lay off and keep firing at the ships laying at their anchors, but when we ware in side we could cut them off, but the batteries on either shore could fire at us. We remained on this station for a fortnight, then we ware releived and sent over to Algiers for cattle for the fleet, and when returning with the cattle, we ware ordered to take the outside station as a look out.

---

[103] *Marquis of Ely*, an armed East Indiaman, was slightly larger than *la Minerve*. She had a total complement of no more than 75 for a voyage in 1801 to the Far East (a fair indication of the numbers needed to weigh anchor and handle the sails) and, on the return journey, twenty of her best men were 'pressed' from her, leaving only 55 to sail her home.

'One morning at 4 A.M. we saw a sail coming bearing down upon us with all sail she could crowd. When drawing nearer we could purceive she mounted 24 guns. We beat to quarter and when they came close to us they hoisted jack, insign, and pennant, Spanish colours. We up English colours and gave hur 6 or 7 guns nearly at one time. Amediate she hall'd hur colours down. They took the fleet inside to be the Spanish fleet and we as a look out ship. We took hur into Adm'l Jarvis and was made fast a stern of his ship but never received anything for hur. She was a rich loaded ship from the River Plate, of South America, which Jervice put into his own pocket.'

Means had to be found to provoke the Spaniards to come out from Cadiz, so a bombardment was started. The following day was the birthday of King George III, traditionally marked by a 21-gun salute. But the salute had to be postponed, so Nelson wrote warning the Spanish of this 'so that the ladies of Cadiz may not be alarmed'. On 3 July *Thunderer*, a bomb vessel (a floating gun platform normally armed with a pair of enormous mortars) was sent in. She was towed into position a mile off shore and proceeded to lob huge explosive shells high up into the sky which rained down onto the town. As expected, although even this did not persuade the Spanish ships to come out and fight, they sallied forth that night with a large number of armed rowing boats.[104] Sometimes referred to as 'gunboats', these were small sailing vessels, usually with one large bow-mounted gun and equipped with long sweeps; convoys were then easy pray for them if the wind dropped. A print in the Naval Chronicle (vol IV) shows the 'sloop of war' HMS *Speedy* being attacked by three or more Spanish gunboats – a single mast, lateen sail and some 16 sweeps – which did not look much smaller than *Speedy*.

To counter this threat, all available ships' boats had been armed to the teeth. Again, Nelson took personal command of one of these rather than remaining on board *Captain*. The hand-to-hand fighting was intense. Nelson's boat was soon spotted and attacked by a far larger boat, 30 men against 13, but Nelson himself fought hand-to-hand like the others in his boat and 18 of the Spaniards attacking him were killed, the rest wounded. Sykes, Nelson's coxswain on *Captain*, acted as his personal bodyguard in the boat action and saved his life. He suffered severe injuries in the process, and a grateful Nelson had him promoted. Two nights later, Nelson sent in *Thunderer* again, this time

---

[104] One of Forester's 'Hornblower' books seemed a little fanciful when he referred to galley-slaves in the Napoleonic era, but several galleys, complete with slaves, were found at Toulon in 1793. At Genoa in 1799, William Hoste 'cut out' a 52-oared galley rowed by 300 slaves, convicts chained to their thwarts until they died, who were glad to assist in her capture. Admiral Keith returned the prisoners, including 250 of the slaves, to the French, who promptly shot them all.

accompanied by two further aptly named 'bombs', *Terror* and *Strombolo*, with considerable effect.

Nelson continued to be dazzled by the thought of the rich pickings to be had at Santa Cruz, and had not abandoned his plans, even though St Vincent had not finally approved of the idea. The reports of the Santa Cruz raid by *Lively* and *Minerve*, and the news that another Spanish treasure galleon was said actually to have arrived there shortly afterwards, made Nelson change his mind. St Vincent had been told by 'a sensible lad' (presumably someone who had returned to the fleet with *la Mutine*) that Santa Cruz could 'be carried with the greatest of ease'. That was enough to convince him that Nelson's ideas were right and so the fateful decision was taken. So, with the approval of Earl St Vincent, Nelson went ahead with the detailed planning for the raid.

At the end of July 1797 his ill-fated raid on Santa Cruz took place. It was totally disastrous. He lost many men killed or badly wounded, but a truce was agreed and the sad remains of his squadron were allowed to return to their ships with full honour, each man fed with bread and with a pint of wine from the Spanish Governor. The officers were first entertained to dinner, but as a social event it was said not to have been a success. Some of the captured British flags are still, to this day, hanging in the church there. Nelson lost his right arm in the fighting, and returned home to recover. When he got back to England, he wrote to Earl St Vincent;

> 'After George Cockburn's gallant action with the *Sabina*, I directed a gold-hilted sword to be made for him, which I had hoped to present to him myself in the most public and handsome manner; but as Providence has decreed otherwise, I must beg of you to present it for me....I feel confident of your goodness.'

After nine months enforced sick leave in England, Nelson returned to duty with the fleet off Cadiz. In May 1798 he was then sent back to Toulon ("Too Long", as the sailors called it) with a squadron of three ships of the line and five frigates. It was known that Napoleon was amassing a large army there, and his orders were to find out what was going on. Nelson spent the next three months searching the Mediterranean for the French fleet, with Napoleon in their midst, just missing them on two occasions. This gives rise to one of the most interesting 'what ifs' in European History. What if Nelson, whose ships were actually seen by the French one night, so close were they, had captured Napoleon then? In August Nelson finally caught up with the French at Aboukir Bay and 'the Battle of the Nile' followed.

Outwardly calm, Nelson was like any other man when it came to excitement, and his 'fin' – the stump of his right arm – would twitch with frustration. Chasing *Genereux* in 1800, Sir Henry Duncan commented that he became fidgety, but nevertheless retained his sense of humour;

> 'Lord Nelson put his head on deck; "Quarter Master, you can put her head a little more to the wind". "No, my Lord". Went down. In a few minutes up again. "Quarter Master, can't you put her head a little more to the wind?" "No, my Lord." Down again. Up again. "Quarter Master, I think you can put her head up a little more to the wind." "No, my Lord." "Then I lie?" "Yes, my Lord." "Then you are a pig."'

The Gibraltar refit had not included renewing *Minerve's* copper bottom so, when she arrived back at the Tagus, St Vincent ordered *Minerve* home to England for a full refit. She joined up with Cockburn's old ship *Meleager* to escort a homeward bound convoy and reached Plymouth in April 1798, 'The Times' reporting;

> 'Plymouth, April 7. Arrived the *Dart* ... from Oporto. She sailed about a month since with 41 sail, under convoy of the *Minerva* and *Meleager* frigates...'

Convoy escort duty was not popular, as their ship's speed had to be that of the slowest old tub in the convoy and (more important to officers and men alike) the chances of prize money were nil. Before departing, Cockburn gave each vessel in the convoy written instructions but, even so, many refused to obey. Captain Ogle in *Meleager* complained that he had had to put a shot ahead of the *Douro*, and then another directly astern of her, and it was not until he put the third shot through her fore-topsail that he got any response – and even then it was only a torrent of abuse!

Tempers became a little frayed, even amongst the officers living cheek by jowl in such confined quarters. A letter to the captain in the Cockburn Papers reads;

> *'La Minerve* March 23rd. 1798
>
> Sir
>
> I beg to request a Court Martial may be held on Mr. John Lamotte, Purser of *La Minerve*, for contempt of me, his superior Officer, & ungentle-manlike conduct on several occasions. Viz. for reflecting on my conduct when acting as first Lieut. of this ship, & for attempting to force me out of his cabin, during the time he was making reflections on my conduct, equally False, & ill founded.
>
> I remain Sir, etc. etc. etc.
>
> J F MALING'

History does not relate whether or not there was a Court Martial; it is more likely that Cockburn, a practical man, banged both their heads together.

At Plymouth, Cockburn soon received orders to proceed to Portsmouth for the promised refit. Unfortunately Nelson had left Spithead in *Vanguard* on 10 April, so Cockburn missed seeing his old friend by a matter of days only.

Interestingly, when undergoing her refit, 'the Minerves' were not all broken up and 'turned over' into other under-manned ships, as would normally have been expected. Instead, most of them remained on her muster roll and were accommodated in the *Prudent* hulk, moored in Portsmouth Harbour. This was because St Vincent had particularly requested that Cockburn should himself return to the fleet with *la Minerve* as soon as ever possible. In the normal run of events, on returning to England he would have been given command of a 'ship of the line', so his admiral's express wish to have him back with the same vessel almost certainly cost him his promotion. Indeed, he would probably have rejoined Nelson, become one of his famous 'band of brothers' and played a leading part at Aboukir Bay. But it also meant that his crew were kept together.

In other respects as well, Cockburn does seem to have had a pretty exceptional crew.[105] This may, in part, be due to so many officers and men following him from *Meleager*, who would have provided a stabilising nucleus. By 1801 only 3 out of 241 men were shown in the muster book as 'prest' but, as we have seen, Samuel and most of his 'volunteer' shipmates in reality had little alternative. In 1798, 126 of her men were rated A.B. and only 39 as ordinary seamen. In common with other ships, *Minerve* usually had three or four punishments a month, but for six consecutive months in 1799 there was not a single punishment, which must be taken to show that her crew were, at the very least, contented with their lot. This was at a time when there was frequent shore leave, and seems to be proof that Cockburn's policy of allowing shore leave whenever possible had paid off.

The work refitting would have been arduous, and many of the crew would therefore have been retained to help the dockyard workforce. But not only was she an unusual ship with an unusual captain and ship's company – another unusual feature was that a few highly trusted members of her crew, including Samuel, were sent on home leave. Partly to minimise disruption, but mainly as a guarantee of their return (a man would not let his mess-mates down and have all further shore leave and other privileges stopped) they were even allowed on shore a few at a time. Samuel was free from 17 May until he returned aboard on

---

[105] R Morriss, 'Cockburn and the British Navy in Transition'.

19 June.

It was a major refit, with a cable tier (so that it was no longer necessary to stow the anchor cable on top of the water-butts) and new decks going in below. She was at the same time re-rated as a '38'. Cockburn had difficulty in persuading the Admiralty that, although now nominally a '38', she needed much more iron ballast on her keel than the normal 38's allowance of 90 tons. Cockburn argued that the new cable tier meant that there was now less room to accommodate shingle and gravel[106] as extra ballast, and that to reduce her total ballast would prejudice her sailing qualities.

The Admiralty disowned ship's figureheads, regarding them as the captains' choice to have or not, as they pleased, or as their pockets would allow. They made no allowance for work on a ship's figurehead, and *la Minerve's* is not shown on her plans at Woolwhich. This is a pity, as the Roman goddess Minerva is normally depicted resplendent with gold helmet and shield; she certainly was on the old *Minerve*, renamed *San Fiorenzo* when she was captured in 1794. *La Minerve's* original French figurehead (indistinctly visible in the print in Jenkins' Naval Achievements, 1817) was probably in a bad state by now, but Cockburn was not without wealth, and it is impossible to imagine that he would have missed this opportunity to have it properly restored.

Whilst *la Minerve* was undergoing her refit, Cockburn arranged for the delivery to Lady Nelson of some Madeira wine that Nelson had sent her. In return, she asked him to take a trunk back to the Mediterranean for her husband, containing cherries in brandy and currant jelly.

After her refit, *Minerve* lay at Spithead waiting to escort a convoy, carrying out routine tasks, 'the People' being kept busy to keep them from getting as bored as the log suggests her officers were;

'Sunday the 23rd September, 1798.
…People employed shifting the Iron Ballast from the Coal hole into ye after gun room…

Monday the 24th September, 1798.
…People employed about the fore and Main rigging … recd. Boatswain & Carpenters stores and 8 Butts of Beer.'

Tuesday the 25th September, 1798.

---

[106] She used to carry 225 tons of it. Water butts were bedded in the gravel in the bottom of the hold to keep them in position.

...People empd. occasionally.[107] Answered signal to take ye guard ... at 8 AM took the Guard, sailed His Majs' Ship *Calypso* with a convoy to the Eastward, Recd. fresh beef 554 lb.

Wednesday the 26th September, 1798.
Fresh breeze and Cloudy weather, People employed occasionally latter part ... recd' Coals from launch.'

Perhaps it was a stroke of luck that the ballast had been shifted from the coal hole before the 'Coals' arrived, and not afterwards!

Next day an unpleasant duty had to be performed. The threat of mutiny cannot have been far from commanders' minds only eighteen months after the 'Great Mutiny' of 1797;

'Thursday the 27th September, 1798.
Fresh breezes ... at 8 AM the signal was made for Punishment at 9 AM hanged 7 Men for mutiny on board H.M.Ship *Defiance*, sent two boats with two Officers to attend at the Punishment. Received fresh beef 422 lb.'

Reminiscent of the causes of the famous Mutiny on the *Bounty*, a similar event took place in 1801. The captain of *Castor* unreasonably ordered his main topsail men repeatedly to reef and unreef the topsail on Christmas Day. The men objected, and a court martial resulted, four men being charged with mutiny. Three were flogged round the fleet, but the fourth was sentenced to be hanged at the yard-arm of his own ship.

'A boat from each ship, with two marines armed in each, was ordered to attend the execution, and I was sent in our boat. A few minutes after he was run up to the yard-arm he began to groan, and soon after so loud that he was heard some distance off. He then struggled and drew up his legs and arms; but as the latter were only fastened above the elbows, he made a shift with his hands to reach the noose of the halter, and pulling it closer, soon expired. Thus it may be said that the poor fellow finished his own existence. The knot of the halter had been placed under his chin instead of being under his ear; it was a great shame that the poor fellow was not lowered down again to put the halter right. When his body had hung for the usual time, it was lowered down and committed to the deep.'[108]

The prospect of more long years away from home was too much for some of *Minerve's* crew. On 19 November, at Portsmouth, a man 'ran', and another followed him the next day, the day she sailed. Both of them (rated as Ordinary

---

107 'Occasionally' does not mean that the crew were idle for most of the time. Far from it, they were kept hard at work at whatever, and whenever, the 'occasion' required.
108 'A Mariner of England', Conway Maritime Press, 1970.

rather than Able Seamen) had entered *Minerve* at the same time as Samuel.

The following nine months were full of frustration and disappointment. The ship had been ready by mid-October but their departure for the Mediterranean was delayed for six weeks whilst the convoy they were to escort southwards was being assembled. At last the convoy was ready and, provisioned for six months and therefore, like all French built frigates, well down in the water,[109] *Minerve* sailed south with the convoy on 20 November.

Earl St Vincent was still C-in-C, Mediterranean when *la Minerve* rejoined Nelson's squadron off Palermo, on 27 December 1798, where the King of Naples and his court had taken refuge and Nelson was under Emma Hamilton's magic spell.

Much had changed in the Mediterranean since Cockburn had been away. Minorca had been recaptured and, of course, Nelson had fought and brilliantly won a complete and resounding victory over the French at Aboukir Bay – the Battle of the Nile. The Mediterranean was no longer their private sea and, although they were still a force to be reckoned with, the British had now established their superiority there.

Cockburn found Nelson, whom he had not seen for some while, a changed man. After his victory of the Nile (which *la Minerve* missed as she was back in England for her refit) he was showered with gifts, foreign titles and universal adulation that seemed to have gone to his head. One of these from the Sultan of Turkey was a *chelengk*, a spray of diamonds to wear in his hat with a star in the centre. The star turned round, driven by a clockwork motor![110]

It must not be forgotten that Nelson had received a severe wound to his forehead, exposing his skull bone for some inch and a half. Current medical opinion is that the blow may have had much the same effect on his brain as the repeated blows to the head that make a boxer 'punch-drunk'. It may well have slightly changed his personality. He himself wrote to Admiral the Earl of St. Vincent, K.B. on 10 August 1798;

> '…Although I keep on, yet I feel that I must soon leave my situation up the Mediterranean to Troubridge… My head is ready to split, and I am always sick; in short, if there is no fracture, my head is severely shaken.'

Lord St Vincent had written to Nelson from Cadiz;

---

[109] Being not quite so sleek, a British frigate was designed to carry a full six months' provisions, whereas French vessels seldom had the need to provision for so long and were designed accordingly.

[110] It was stolen from the National Art Collection in the 1950s and broken up.

'Tell Lady Hamilton I rely on her to administer to your health at Naples, where I have no doubt it will soon be re-established.'

She did.

Cockburn, ever loyal to his old friend and former mentor, never uttered a word against Nelson. But he did, much later, confide in a friend who had enquired about Nelson's character;

'He is a curious compound of weakness, with power of high exertions, of intrepidity and talent; and blessed with a never failing kindness of heart.'[111]

It was commonly said that an officer's marriage vows did not extend beyond Gibraltar and, to his brother officers' regret, Nelson had already been cavorting earlier with his 'dolly' in Leghorn – openly and even in front of his step-son, Fanny Nelson's son Josiah Nisbet, who was one of his midshipmen. By now he was rapidly coming under the thrall of Lady Hamilton. Writing to her from his ship, and using a pseudonym for himself, he wrote;

'I dare say twins will again be the fruit of your and his meeting… Have the dear thatched cottage[112] ready to receive him…'

An entry in the journal of John Moore (later the hero of Corunna) for 15 July 1800, written at Leghorn, where he had met the British Ambassador, reads;

'Sir Wm. and Lady Hamilton were then attending the Queen of Naples. Lord Nelson was there attending upon lady Hamilton. He is covered with stars, ribbons, and medals, more like the Prince of an Opera than the Conqueror of the Nile. It is really melancholy to see a brave and good man, who has deserved well of his country, cutting so pitiful a figure.'

It was during this unsatisfactory period that Samuel was yet again taken and held as a prisoner, presumably of the French, for nearly twelve weeks. Cockburn had been sent to Leghorn, where he was to meet a representative of the Austrian army and talk with him about military aid. Whilst there he attempted (unsuccessfully, it seems) to negotiate an exchange of prisoners of war with the French. Meanwhile Cockburn had been ordered to join the frigate *Santa Theresa* and, with two sloops attached to him;

'to cruise off Genoa City and Cape Delle Melle to prevent vessels entering Genoese ports with provisions … and to cruise one month on this service.'

Following these orders, Cockburn captured three small vessels and effectively silenced shore batteries at Diano. Then he took two more small vessels off San

---

[111] Quoted by R Morriss. Letter from Cockburn to J.Croker, 11 April 1845, NMM CKE/6.
[112] A reference, not to some snug little love nest, but in the then current vernacular to that particular portion of her anatomy that most endeared her to him.

Remo and destroyed two forts at Porto Mauritio before rejoining Nelson at Palermo. In addition *Minerve* was involved in the capture by Lord Keith's fleet of three frigates and two brigs in June 1799, but Samuel (being absent from muster) did not qualify for a share of the prize money.

All *La Minerve's* muster book shows is that Samuel was captured on 3 May 1799 and that he was returned to her on 26 July. The captain's journal mentions no encounter with the enemy on 3 May and is of no assistance. Possibly Samuel was a member of a prize crew put onboard a prize that was recaptured by the French off Leghorn. The only clue we get is this entry in the log on the day he was returned;

> 'Friday the 26th July 1799 ... several Strange Sails in Sight ... at ½ past 5 ans'd ye private Sig'l to a Man of War. Showed our pendants to ye *Seahorse* Frigate. Made No 9 General ... hove to and spoke H.M.*Seahorse* at 8 ... at 10 hoisted ye Jolly Boat up and filled...'

Minerve was at sea all that day. According to her muster book, that was the date when Samuel rejoined his ship, so one must assume it was to recover him that the jolly boat was sent across to *Seahorse*.

Samuel's capture and return coincide with one of the more unfortunate episodes in Nelson's career. Captain Foote of the *Seahorse* found himself Senior Naval Officer in the Bay of Naples at a time when the loyal Neapolitan army and their Turkish and Russian allies had the French and their revolutionary Neapolitan supporters on the run. The King had delegated full powers to Cardinal Ruffo, and Captain Foote felt he had to take orders from Ruffo, as Nelson's instructions to him were to do as the king told him. At the cardinal's request he therefore counter-signed the terms for a surrender that Ruffo and the Russian allies had agreed, under which the disaffected Neapolitans who held two forts overlooking the bay would be transported to France and the French in another fort had, it seems, been offered similar terms. They were ready to leave when Nelson arrived. He tore up he surrender terms (which Captain Foote had considered to be unnecessarily generous) and sent many of the French and their Neapolitan friends to their deaths. Shortly after, Admiral Caracciolo was found in peasant's garb and he, too, was hanged for siding with the revolutionary Neapolitans against their lawful king.

Perhaps Samuel Blackmore had been held as a prisoner in the Bay of Naples and was released, as part of the surrender that Nelson abrogated, and put on *Seahorse*. All we know for certain of Samuel's part in all this is that, as well as losing his share of the prize money for the prizes taken in his absence, he again lost his pay whilst absent from muster. But Samuel was either wise or he was lucky; unlike many others, he was never charged 15s [75p] for 'venerials' – the cost of medicines to treat 'the pox'.[113]

The news now reached Palermo, where *la Minerve* next went, that the French Admiral Bruix, with 25 ships of the line, had evaded the blockade of Brest. He had passed Gibraltar on 5 May, and was now at large in the Mediterranean. It was understood that he was to rendezvous with a Spanish fleet comprising another 17 ships of the line – a major threat, as that would mean a fleet of more than forty ships, if they could meet up, opposing the British fleet.

By June 1799, St Vincent had become exhausted and was not well. He handed over command to his second-in-command Lord Keith and in July he sailed for England. Nelson wrote to him;

'We have a report that you are going home. This distresses us most exceedingly, and myself in particular ... I wish not to detract from the merits of whoever may be your successor, but it must take a length of time ... to be in any manner a St Vincent. We look up to you, as we have always found you, as to our father, under whose fostering care we have been led to fame ... be again our St Vincent and we shall be happy.'

Nelson's sentiments were sincerely felt. It is sad to relate, therefore, that later events changed their mutual feelings of respect into hostility. Nelson did not fight shy of going to court if necessary, and in 1803 he claimed, and won, £20,000 prize money from his former commanding officer – money that St Vincent had obtained as his 'Flag eighths' as C-in-C Mediterranean at a time when he was, in reality, back home on sick leave. Nelson, his feelings of warmth now evaporated, had written;

'My Commander-in-Chief runs away with all the money I fought for... But damn me if I let any man swindle me out of my property whilst he is at ease in England... I have only justice, honour, and the custom of the service on my side; he has partiality, power, money and rascality on his'.[114]

Lord Keith, taking over from St Vincent as Commander-in-Chief in the Mediterranean, was naturally concerned to track Bruix down before he could meet up with the Spanish fleet, and Cockburn joined in the hunt. It was unsuccessful, but anything was better to Cockburn than kicking his heels in Palermo.

---

[113] "Five minutes with Venus, and six months with Mercury", as the saying went.
[114] 'Nelson: A Personal History', by Christopher Hibbert, p236.

In September 1799 Nelson ordered Cockburn[115] to rejoin the Lisbon station (the most prize-rich waters that Nelson was able to send him to) under Rear-Admiral Duckworth. Much of the time was taken up with routine work, as Cockburn found himself Senior Naval Officer there. For the next 17 months, based mainly on Lisbon and the River Tagus, they patrolled up and down in the Atlantic gales from Cape Finisterre on the north western tip of France, down across the Bay of Biscay to Cadiz and back up again.

Many minor and some major prizes were taken, each needing a prize crew to take her into a friendly port. *La Minerve's* crew was also being badly depleted by sickness and death. The crew's health continued to be a problem, as Cockburn explains in a letter to Rear-Admiral Duckworth, his new commanding officer;

'La Minerve in the Tagus Oct 22nd 1799

Sir

Since my parting with you on the 17th Inst, twenty of the Crew of His Majesty's Ship under my Command, have been taken ill with Scorbutic eruptions, attended with a contageous Fever, of which one Man died this Morning, & two are now given over by the Surgeon. I therefore determined to anchor at this Place (which owing to Northerly Winds, & a very heavy Sea, I have only just been able to fetch) to purchase some Lemons & fresh Provisions, which my Surgeon represents as absolutely neceſsary to check this disorder in its infancy, having obtained these, I shall proceed without a moments loſs of time to execute your Order, & I trust the above circum-stances will appear to you sufficient to authorize my conduct herein…'

In another letter, also addressed 'To Jno. Thos. Duckworth Esq Rear Admiral of the White etc.. etc.. etc.' Cockburn reports;

'La Minerve at Sea 9th Nov 1799

Sir

I have the honor [sic] to inform you, that His Majesty's Ship under my Command, captured last Night (Lat 42-Long 11'0") *La Mouche* French Ship Privateer of 20 Guns, & 145 men, belonging to Bordeaux, out twelve days, but had made no capture.

> I have the Honor to be
> Sir
> your most Obdt. Servt.
> G.COCKBURN.'

---

[115] This was the last time that the two friends were to meet during the war, although they frequently met (mainly at Cockburn's London house) afterwards, during the Peace of Amiens, to discuss prize money.

H.M. Frigate 'MINERVE', *38 guns, (Captain George Cockburn, R.N.) leaving the Tagus, 1797, by T. Butterworth*

It is difficult for us, in our centrally heated houses and from the comfort of our fireside armchairs, to imagine the terrible conditions in which *Minerve's* officers and men lived during this period, not just occasionally or for brief moments of time only, but continually. Men were dying of scurvy, rheumatism was rife, the gales continued and there was no let-up. It was equally hard on the ship herself.

Cockburn reported on his work to Admiral Duckworth in December 1799;

> 'I proceeded with the *St Vincent* schooner to reconnoitre Ferrol and Corunna off which place I arrived last night and immediately sent my first lieutenant on board the schooner with orders to stand close in under the lighthouse and at daylight to hoist American colours and endeavour to get a Spanish pilot on board of him, which he effected and by which he was enabled to run close into the harbour of Corunna, where there are only two French privateers...'

The financial rewards of the prizes they captured (off Cape Finisterre was a happy hunting ground for a frigate) cannot have compensated them for their privations. On 21 January 1800 Cockburn wrote to Admiral Duckworth about the past four weeks;

> 'After parting with you on the 23 Decr. last, to see the Spanish Brig *Volcano* into the Tagus, I met with nothing but strong SW Winds, against which it was with the utmost difficulty, after carrying away three Hawsers, and a

117

stream Cable towing her, that I got far enough to the Southward to fetch in on the evening of the 5th of January; *La Minerve* having sprung her Fore Topmast the night before, and split most of her Sails, I thought it prudent, it then blowing a gale of Wind from the Westward, to anchor also for the night, during which we shifted our Fore Topmast, & repaired our Sails, & were ready for Sea again in the Morning; but the Gale continuing to the SW it was impoſsible to get out, & excepting for a few hours on the 10th which were moderate, (& during which we got very nearly to the Bar, tho' forced by the old sea & Gale to go back again) we have had inceſsant Gale from SW to West till today; there have been several veſsels lost attempting to run in during the Gale, & I fear several are English Newfoundland Ships.

I found in the Tagus the *Mondore* Brig captain Selby, who had Orders from Lord Keith to put himself under my Command; I have not however myself received any Orders from His Lordship…'

Whilst in England the New Year and the New Century were being welcomed in[116] with traditional revelry, Samuel and his shipmates were out in the boats, trying to tow their ship into harbour through tempestuous winter Atlantic gales and then, during the night, mending sails and spars in readiness for the next day.

Further letters from Captain Cockburn to his superiors, passed on by them to the Admiralty and reproduced in the London Gazette and the Naval Chronicle, report the taking of *Le Furet*, a French privateer (and the recapture of her prize, the *Alert* from North Yarmouth) in March 1800 and, that September, three more fully-laden merchant vessels off Cape Finisterre. *Minerve's* prizes included *la Caroline*, a 16 gun privateer, three more privateers totalling 49 guns taken in 1800. A copy of a letter to Lord Keith is amongst Cockburn's papers;

'*La Minerve* at Sea 16th April 1800

My Lord

I have the honor to inform your Lordship, His majesty's Ship under my Command captured this day *La Vengeance* French Privateer belonging to Rochelle, of 15 Guns, & 130 men, sailed yesterday from Vigo, since which

---

[116] In fact they were not. *The Times* for 26 December 1799 thundered;
'We have uniformly rejected all letters and declined all discussion upon the question of when the present century ends, as it is one of the most absurd that can engage the public attention, and we are astonished to find it has been the subject of so much dispute, since it is plain. The present century will not terminate till January 1, 1801, unless it can be made out that 99 are 100… It is a silly, childish discussion, and only exposes the want of brains of those who maintain a contrary opinion…'
On 1 January 1801 a leading article in *The Times* said;
'At the beginning of a NEW YEAR and the opening of another Century, it would have been grateful to have announced the return of PEACE…'

she has not made any Capture – during her former cruise, she took the Veſsels as per margin.'

A marginal note lists the British vessels taken. This was followed shortly after by another report to Lord Keith;

'As your Lordship may not have received my letters on this Subject, I send per margin a list of the Privateers taken by His Majesty's Ship under my Command since cruising off this Coast.'

The marginal note listed *La Mouche*, 20 guns, *Le Furet*, 16 guns, *La Vengeance*, 15 guns (a little unusual to have an odd number) and *Northa Signora del Carmine*, 1 gun.

CHAPTER 8

On 1 January 1801, when he was still 24 – the day that the new Union Flag[117] (which is wrongly called the Union Jack) was adopted – Samuel was promoted Coxswain of *Minerve*. Each ship had one Coxswain, a petty officer paid at the same rate as the Boatswain's Mates and the Yeomen of the Sheets – from £2.2.6 [£2.12] to £1.16.6 [£1.82] per lunar month, according to the 'rating' – the size of the ship – and *Minerve* was only a 'fifth rate'.

Of more importance than his monthly pay, particularly in a successful frigate, was a Coxswain's share of any prize money. One eighth of the value of every vessel captured was divided between the midshipmen, petty officers (including the Coxswain) and marine sergeants as prize money. This was obviously worth a great deal more than the quarter share, divided between them all, that the other common sailors and marines got; depending on the numbers, a petty officer's share could be worth five or six times as much.

The Coxswain was in charge of the captain's own boat – his 'barge'. A Coxswain was:

> 'The officer who steers a boat, and has command of the boat's crew, and all things belonging to it. He has a whistle to call and encourage his men, and must be ready with his crew to man the boat on all occasions; he sits at the stern of the boat, and steers.'[118]

Samuel had, by then, a great deal of experience in small boats, first pulling an oar (possibly graduating to 'stroke oar') and then, probably, acting as coxswain of one of the other boats (not a petty officer's appointment) before being promoted Coxswain to have charge of the captain's barge.

In the absence of refrigeration, live animals and poultry for the officers' table were often kept in the ship's boats, so his duties as coxswain of one of the other boats before he was promoted could at times have been a little unpleasant! But the captain's own barge, used for taking him on shore or to pay formal visits to the captains of other ships, would hardly have been used for this purpose.

---

117 Until then it was simply the red Cross of St George for England, with the white diagonal St Andrew's cross on a blue ground for Scotland superimposed on it – the same as the present flag but without the diagonal red cross for Ireland.
118 W Burley, Universal Dictionary of the Marine, 1815 p92.

Being Coxswain in charge of the captain's personal transport was a highly prized position. On the lower deck, information, gossip and news were scarce commodities. Taking the captain to dinner on the admiral's flagship was an occasion when the coxswain and his boat's crew were entertained by the 'host' ship,[119] and thus they would have been the first to return to *Minerve* with all the latest tittle-tattle, rumours and gossip. As a result, the coxswain would have been a popular man. Besides, he was a trusted man, trusted not to 'run', and would have had the chance to go on shore from time to time whilst he was waiting for his captain's return. His food would have been the same as before but (depending on what accommodation was available) he may have been able to sling his hammock in a more comfortable place.

As a petty officer, a Coxswain could sometimes be put in quite a difficult position, as he was frequently asked by the officers to report on what was being said below decks. In a mutiny (as in the case of the *Blanche*) he often took the side of the men rather than the officers. Like Sykes (Nelson's coxswain on *Captain*) he was usually more of a personal servant than a petty officer and, rather like a chauffeur today, spent much of his time ferrying his captain around the rest of the fleet in his personal 'barge'. The crew of the captain's barge were all picked men – partly because they could be trusted not to 'run' whilst on shore – and most captains liked their bargemen to be well dressed (the beginnings of a uniform for men on the lower deck) so that he could himself cut a bit of a dash when visiting other ships. Depending on the captain's personality, the coxswain and he probably got to know one another quite well – an unusual relationship in the Navy where the gulf between officers and men was unbridgeable.

During *Minerve's* 1798 refit at Portsmouth, Cockburn had a special launch made for her, larger than the normal frigate's launch, but specially designed for attacking larger vessels – a wise move that paid off later on. A frigate's launch, a heavy-weight work-horse, was normally some 28-32 ft long, and had eight or ten oarsmen. This launch, extra-long for a frigate's launch, would probably have been 32 ft or more long and had ten oars.

On a 'cutting out' expedition, the launch (often pictured as being under sail – like all ship's boats it was fully equipped for sailing) was by tradition in the charge of the First Lieutenant, and was always the first into action. Most launches were fitted with a carronade in the bows, many having slides that

---

[119] See, for example, Wetherell's 1804 account of life in the frigate *Hussar*, and as a member of her boat's crew, in 'The Adventures of John Wetherell' (edited by C.S.Forester.)

enabled them to be stowed in the bottom of the boat when not in use.

When visiting other ships, Samuel gave hand signals as they approached, signifying he had a 'Post-Captain' with him, so that the 'host' vessel could arrange for the necessary guard of honour to welcome him coming up over the side. On returning to his own ship with Cockburn, he was challenged by the marine sentry as he approached the side. By tradition, as he had the ship's own captain in his launch, he simply answered '*la Minerve*'.

All through the long winter of 1800/1801 *la Minerve* continued to battle her way through the Atlantic winter gales on blockade duty, whilst the enemy were nice and snug in port. With all this exceptionally hard work undertaken by *Minerve*, the ship was again soon worn out, leaking badly[120] and in urgent need of repair. Long and sleek she may have been, and fast too, but *Minerve* was not able to withstand the battering of the elements as well as a fractionally slower but more solidly-built British designed '36'. She was also probably much more uncomfortable to sail in, as frigates of French design tended to pitch badly. The sailing qualities of other Coulomb-designed frigates of the *Minerve* class were said to be;

> 'Responsive to their helm, carried their sail excellently, but in anything like a seaway they pitched and lost speed; for all that, both their pitching and rolling motions were easy. They were indifferent sailers close-hauled, much better on a reach, and below average with the wind astern. They steered well, tending neither to gripe nor to be slack, and they were quick in stays both tacking and veering.'[121]

Teams of men were forced to man the pumps round the clock, day in, day out, until they could get the ship re-caulked and water-tight again. Lisbon, on the River Tagus, had the necessary facilities, so Cockburn now sailed for the Tagus with orders to join Rear-Admiral Warren, off Cadiz, as soon as he could. Cockburn wrote to Sir John Warren Bart. K.B., Rear-Admiral of the White, from the Tagus on 14th January 1801;

> 'Sir
>
> I arrived at this Place on the 7th inst. after a long & bad cruise off Cape Finistere, making about 16 Inches of Water an hour, with rigging, sails etc. in a very bad condition…
>
> I have obtained a Party of Calkers from the Dock Yard here, & am using

---

[120] Some years previously Nelson remarked that, under similar conditions on *Agamemnon*, not a man had slept dry for weeks.

[121] Jean Baudriot, The History of the French Frigate 1650-1850 (Rotherfield, 1993) p192.

every exertion to get *La Minerve* ready for Service again, & immediately that is effected, I will pursuant to your Order, join you off Cadiz.

I have the honour to be

Sir

your very humble Servt.

G.COCKBURN.'

La Minerve was in dry dock for more than a fortnight with teams of local caulkers swarming all over her deck and sides re-caulking her seams, from 25 to 32 of them, all faithfully recorded each day in the log. Shore leave would have been granted to the more trust-worthy members of her crew, and Samuel (who now had privileges as a petty officer) would inevitably have been one of them. As a member of the captain's barge's crew he would also have had plenty of opportunities for visiting the town. He would have cut quite a dash on shore; Cockburn was a wealthy young man, son of a well-connected family, Nelson's protégé and used to entertaining. He had the means to have his 'barge' crew dressed to impress and, as Senior Naval Officer in Lisbon, we must assume that he did so. Samuel's uniform (and that of the rest of the captain's barge's crew) when engaged on his captain's work, would have consisted of white duck trousers, a short dark blue jacket, with big shiny brass buttons, over his check 'slop' shirt, a black silk scarf and a black hat with a ribbon.

It was at Lisbon that an event happened which, in later life, Samuel must have looked back on as the high point of his naval service;

> 'Thursday the 15th January, 1801. Moderate breezes & Cloudy. People emp'd about the Rigging … 30 caulkers emp'd caulking the Ship. Arrived here *H.M.S. Endymion* with His Royal Highness Prince Augustus[122] aboard, fired a salute of 21 guns when she came to anchor and 21 at do. when his Royal Highness went on the Shore.'

We can imagine Cockburn stepping down into his 'barge', its crew in their best uniforms, to be rowed over to *Endymion* to dine with His Royal Highness. It must have been with the greatest possible pride that Samuel took his accustomed place in the sternsheets, his captain wearing his best uniform and carrying the ceremonial sword given to him by Nelson after the *Sabina* affair – but standing behind his captain, holding the tiller, and not sitting beside him!

The caulking continued, and presumably the saluting, too;

> 'Monday the 19th January 1801. 32 caulkers emp'd caulking the Ship … sailed *H.M.S Endymion*.'

---

[122] Duke of Sussex, George III's son.

124

No sooner had *Minerve* been laid up than Admiral Ganteaume led a squadron of seven French ships of the line, accompanied by two frigates, out of Brest, having managed to evade the British blockade there. They were sighted off Cape Finisterre by the British frigate *Concorde*, which had taken over whilst *Minerve* was out of commission. *Success* took up the chase and shadowed the French down the Atlantic coast and on into the Mediterranean. Each time she came too close for their liking, two of the fastest sailing French ships put about and made for her. Each time this happened she was forced to turn and flee. Finally, she had the misfortune to be taken by surprise by a fluke wind, they caught up with her and she was forced to surrender.

As soon as she was ready again, *Minerve* sailed south for Cadiz to rejoin the fleet and warn Admiral Warren that the French squadron was out. Her departure on 1 February 1801 required more work of Samuel and the ship's boats;

'Sunday the 1st February 1801. Got under way down the Tagus at ½ past 5, let go the best Bower Anchor, parted the Cable in bringing the Ship up, the [?freshes] running very strong down, lost the Anchor and 135 fthms of Cable, let go the small Bower Anchor and brought the ship up. Ranged the stearn [sic] cable … all the Boats emp'd creeping for the Anchor and Cable but without Effect.'

It is interesting to see how the war at sea was going from Napoleon's point of view;[123]

'To General Berthier, Minister of War.
Paris, 27th Pluviôse, Year IX.
(16 February 1801)

I beg you will inform General Brune that I am extremely displeased with the conduct of General Clément at Leghorn; that by his carelessness, he has compromised the safety of the ship *Regulus*; that he has permitted English officers to enter the Port of Leghorn under a flag of truce, received them at dinner, and allowed them to remain several days in the town, which is against all regulations; and that I have been pained to see that French Generals could forget the outrages with which the English never cease to overwhelm our prisoners.'

Ganteaume's intention had been to reinforce Napoleon's army in Egypt but, on hearing that Lord Keith was already there, he decided instead to put into Toulon. Cockburn was a couple of days sailing behind the French when he entered the Mediterranean. As he did not know for certain where they were

---

[123] 'New Letters of Napoleon I omitted from the Edition published under the Auspices of Napoleon III, From the French by Lady Mary Loyd', Heinemann, London, 1903.

bound, his task in tailing them was not easy. He suspected, however, that Toulon was where he would find them so, leaving his two escorting frigates to keep watch there, he pressed on for Minorca to find Warren, capturing the *Glommen* (a Danish brig of 20 guns and a crew of 100) on the way. Napoleon was pleased with Ganteaume, and also that Murat had undone all Nelson's good work at Naples, writing to his brother in Madrid;

> 'To Citizen Lucien Bonaparte, Ambassador at Madrid.
> Paris, 9th Ventôse, Year IX.
> (28th February 1801)
>
> Rear-Admiral Ganteaume reached Toulon on 30th Pluviôse [19 February], having taken two English corvettes and one English frigate… Whatever it may cost, we must become masters of the Mediterranean, or force the English to efforts which they will not long be able to continue.
>
> General Murat, commanding the Army of Observation in the South, concluded an armistice … with the King of the two Sicilies, by the terms of which that Prince has laid an embargo on all English and Turkish ships.'

It was just Samuel's bad luck that, whilst he was *Minerve's* Coxswain, the heady days of prize taking seemed to be over. During that period they only took two prizes – the *Glommen*, and the French merchantman that was part of Ganteaume's convoy. Unfortunately, the embargo on Danish ships and their cargoes was lifted only a few weeks later, so *Glommen* was probably disallowed as a lawful prize of war.

Warren, instead of laying a proper blockade on Toulon, left it to *Minerve* and the other two frigates for a whole month without going there himself or even sending another ship to help with the blockade. It was hardly surprising, therefore, that on 19 March, in a heavy gale again, Ganteaume slipped out of Toulon with a convoy of seven merchant vessels just as *Pearl*, one of Cockburn's escorting frigates, was struggling with broken topmasts.

Two more letters from Napoleon to his brother in Madrid cast a further light on his knowledge of naval affairs;

> 'To Citizen Lucien Bonaparte, Ambassador at Madrid
> Paris, 27th Ventôse, Year IX
> (18 March 1801)
>
> The English have hardly any garrison at Port Mahon. If the Spanish would stir themselves a little at Cadiz and at other ports, the island might be seized, at some moment when their squadron is engaged in another part of the Mediterranean.'

'To Citizen Lucien Bonaparte, Ambassador at Madrid
Paris, 27th Floréal, Year IX
(15th May 1801)

Set the Court of Madrid against the Pope, by informing it, as a certainty, that, at the request of Paul I, and without consulting any other power, he has re-established the Jesuits. The Pope is an honest man, but narrow-minded...

Admiral Bruix is on the point of starting with five vessels and five frigates, laden with troops to be landed, and will appear before Cadiz. I desire the five Spanish vessels shall be put under his orders....Take all necessary measures for enabling the five ships which are at Cadiz to join the French squadron which will appear before that place, and act according to circumstances, either making an incursion into the Mediterranean, or turning back, if necessary, to proceed to the East or West Indies...

Further, you will keep profound secrecy as to this movement of Admiral Bruix....'

Ganteaume would have escaped entirely if Cockburn, suspicious at the suddenly increased activity in Toulon's harbour, had not been on his guard. On 19 March he was lucky enough to pick up a straggler from the French convoy. Her crew confirmed his suspicion that they were bound for Alexandria in Egypt, so he detached *Pearl* to inform Lord Keith (Commander-in-Chief, Mediterranean) and set off to find his own immediate commanding officer, Warren, again.

But Warren, cast in the mould of Hotham rather than Nelson, did not believe in informing his captains of his plans, let alone consulting with them. He had not even thought fit to leave any message for *la Minerve* saying where he had gone, or even suggesting a possible rendezvous, so Cockburn was faced with yet more guess work. He must have been furious with his commanding officer for his incompetence, but worse was to come. The search wasted several days. It was not until 10 April that he found Warren half way between Malta and Alexandria. He was astonished to hear that Warren had not only sighted the French ships off Sardinia, but had actually managed to lose them again.

La Minerve had another quick look for Ganteaume herself before heading off for Alexandria, where she came under the direct orders of Lord Keith. Keith, hearing Cockburn's news of the French convoy's intentions and being worried about Ganteaume's approach which posed a direct threat to his own transports in Aboukir Bay, issued his orders to Cockburn;

'The French have an idea to land men to the westward ... therefore be so good as to look out as close inshore as is safe about 20 leagues to the west-ward for five days and then return here if you do not see them. Take care, I fear they have got our signals.'

Keith then sent *Minerve* back to Minorca, where her next assignment was to escort an enormous convoy from Minorca with vital supplies and reinforcement to the army in Egypt. She arrived at Mahon on 16 June 1801, but was not able to get in, the captain's log explaining;

> '...launch Watering ... got under Way, but it falling Calm and the Boats not being able to tow the ship a head was obliged to Anchor again.'

It was not until the following day, 17 June, that the wind picked up again and they were able to drop anchor in Port Mahon, 'the People' being kept busy painting the ship inside and out.

It was at Mahon that Samuel suffered a personal disaster. On 16 June 1801, he was again reduced to A.B., but the log gives us no idea why. The extract above merely indicates that Samuel, in charge of the ship's boats, must have had a gruelling day as Coxswain.

So what happened on 16 June? We can only guess. It cannot have been 'over indulgence' whilst on shore, or failing to return from shore leave, as they were still at sea that day. It is possible that Samuel was 'broken' for some infraction of naval discipline such as drunkenness on board, but there is no mention in the log of his ever receiving punishment. Maybe he was reprimanded for not succeeding in getting *Minerve* into harbour with the boats that day, and answered back, which would be 'contempt' or 'insolence to a superior officer'. But let's be charitable and assume that he was injured – perhaps a rope parted and something heavy fell on him – and that he could no longer carry on as Coxswain.

La Minerve left Minorca, with her charges, on 23 June. This time, thanks to the boredom of convoy duty, the delights of shore leave at Mahon and the watering parties there were soon forgotten. The crew's morale deteriorated rapidly;

> 'Monday 6 July; At 12 punish'd Patk. White (marine) with 3 doz lashes for Drunkenness & Wm Day (ditto) with 3 Dozn. for neglect of duty, Jas. Hutchinson (Seaman) with 1 doz & Rb. Shankey with 2 Do for Contempt.'

Convoy duty was unpopular with officers and men alike. It was not what, in their view, a crack frigate should be doing – taking prizes. Admiralty regulations even expressly forbade leaving a convoy to chase a potential prize. Samuel was probably caught up in the general feeling of discontent in the ship, but his demotion came before the convoy duty started, so that cannot have been the reason for his downfall. It was essential to keep the 'People' busy at times like this, so there was much scrubbing of decks and they were kept fully employed on repairing the rigging, mending sails and other routine work.

If it was difficult to maintain discipline amongst the men, keeping any semblance of order amongst the masters of the merchant ships (most of whom seemed quite incapable of keeping close together for their own safety) was almost impossible. *Minerve's* aim was to remain to windward of the convoy, from where she could swoop down onto any would-be attacker, but this was not always possible. The captain's journal gives the clear impression that Captain Cockburn was feeling the frustration and strain of convoy duty just as much as the rest of his ship's company;

> 'Fired gun at merchantman for going ahead of the rest. Fired shot at one of
> the convoy to make her obey signal ... ditto ... to make her keep her station
> ... took one of convoy in tow, being astern of the convoy...'

And yet convoy duty was not without reward to flag officers and captains. Merchants, city guilds and even Lloyds were generous in expressing their gratitude for convoys brought safely home. They could also earn between one and two per cent 'freight money' on the value of gold, silver and specie entrusted on homeward voyages to their care. Lord Keith is said to have earned £67,000 in the two years to November 1801 by this means[124].

La Minerve reached Aboukir Bay with her convoy on 17 July 1801. Here she was ordered by Lord Keith to return to Warren's squadron off Taranto, calling at Elba and Tuscany on the way to see if he could find any trace of Ganteaume. The log tells us;

> 'Friday the 7th August 1801. Departed this Life John Smart belonging to
> H.M Ship *Foudroyant...*
>
> 'Saturday the 8th August 1801 ... committed the Body of the Deceased to
> the Deep.'

Minerve presumably took on board sailors who had been wounded whilst on shore at Alexandria with the army in Sir Sidney Smith's Naval Brigade, as there is no mention of how John Smart came to be on her.

On Monday 24 August Patrick White, marine, again received a dozen lashes for neglect of duty and four others got the same treatment for both neglect and drunkenness. The unfortunate White must have had a remarkably thick skin both to deserve, and to be able to take, so much punishment!

It took *la Minerve* three weeks to reach Malta, due to contrary winds and yet more storm damage. Cockburn knew he would no longer find Warren at Taranto by then, so he sailed instead for Leghorn. On the way he fell in with two

---

124 N.A.M.Rogers, The Wooden World: An Anatomy of the Georgian Navy.

British frigates *Phoenix* and *Pomone* on 2 September 1801. Some while after they had parted company, *la Minerve* saw two French frigates, *Succès* and *Bravoure*. Firing signal guns to the other two frigates (by then only just visible) to attract their attention, she gave chase. The enemy were making for Leghorn. Attempting to go about in a hurry, *Succès* 'missed stays' and ran aground. *Minerve's* log reads;

> 'Shortened sail and hove to off the northern end of Elba SW 4 or 5 miles. At 4.30 made sail. Two strange sail to the N.E. standing towards us. At 5.30 made the private signal which was not answered... Made the signal to HM Ships *Phoenix* and *Pomone*, the enemy in sight. Fired several guns before the signal was answered. At ½ past 7 bore up in chase; made all sail. At ½ past 9 came up with the *Success* French frigate which had stuck on the shoal off Vada. Fired one shot when she struck her colours. Made signal to the *Pomone* the ship on shore had struck but we had not taken possession of her. Still in chase of the other frigate [*Bravoure*, 42 guns] beating up towards Leghorne; fired at the French frigate as we passed on opposite tacks. The enemy ran ashore under the batteries of Lonlivera when her fore and main-mast went by the board. At ½ past 5 after much firing she struck her colours. Out all boats and sent them with the 1st and 3rd lieutenants to set her on fire but finding a number of prisoners onboard that could not get away owing to the surf on the beach, the boats were obliged to return with the captain, first lieutenant, and as many more of the prisoners as they could bring. Sent the boats for more prisoners but the night coming on and the heavy fire from the batteries, and soldiers on the beach, was forced to quit the prize and return onboard. Boats hoisted. At 9, filled and stood off.'

The *Succès* was the British frigate *Success* which had had the misfortune to be captured by the French some months previously. Next day a party got her off with *Minerve's* launch, and a prize crew of 30 men were put on board to sail her back to Port Mahon. A nice legal point arises here. Is one of His Majesty's Ships, taken by the enemy, used by them and then recaptured, properly a 'prize'? The answer, fortunately for *Minerve's* officers and men, is that she is.

After a few more days, and with 158 prisoners on board, *Minerve* chased and took a Genoese vessel before reaching Mahon on 11 September. There, her prisoners were put on a prison ship and *Success* was taken safely into port.

Cockburn eventually received a belated letter of thanks from Warren, his commanding officer. Giving praise and thanks for a good job well done did not, it seems, come easily to Sir John;

'*Renown*, Mahon, 26th Oct 1801

Sir,

Having received the Commander in Chief's direction to communicate to you his Thanks & Appreciation for the activity & exertion manifested by you in the recapture of His Majesty's Ship *Success*, & destruction of *La Bravoure* French Frigate -

I am happy in conveying the same to you, & request you will accept of my thanks also, upon the above important service...'

One gains the impression that, writing to him like this, Warren was probably mindful of Cockburn's obvious feeling of antipathy. Cockburn was hardly likely to forget Warren's loss of Ganteaume's fleet and his general inactivity and conduct earlier that year which had wasted so much of Cockburn's time trying to find him. Warren (who, earlier in his career, had earned the public's respect as a frigate captain and had received a glowing write-up in the Naval Chronicle) seems to have 'gone off' in later years, suffering no doubt from what we would nowadays call 'executive burnout'. He is described in delightfully dismissive terms in one of the standard biographies;[125]

'Memory of him has grown dim except perhaps in his native county where a public house in Nottingham still bears his name.'

As C. Northcote Parkinson puts it, in the context of the 1812 war against America, when Cockburn again found himself under Warren;

'Sir John Borlase Warren ... had been distinguished as a frigate captain but he may have been worn out by the time he hoisted his flag... Greater energy and ruthlessness were shown by his second-in-command, Rear Admiral Sir George Cockburn.[126]

The Mistral blows unremittingly for four or five days at a time, when even the dogs walk with their tails down. That September, in the teeth of the Mistral's icy blast, they were again on blockade duty off Toulon, when rumours of peace negotiations reached them. On 24 October a French brig under flag of truce confirmed that peace had been declared. They even invited *Minerve* to enter Toulon harbour, but Cockburn politely declined the invitation. Again, the log gives no idea of the jubilation on board as the news flashed round the lower deck;

'Monday the 25th October 1801. Spoke a French Man of War Brig from Toulon.'

---

125 Quoted in Pack, 'The Man who burned the White House'.
126 'Britannia Rules', Royal Naval Museum, Portsmouth, 1977.

Cockburn decided to return to Mahon where, to his horror, Admiral Warren, anxious to return home as quickly as possible, hoisted his admiral's flag on *Minerve*. The captain's journal reads;

> 'Thursday 5th November 1801 ... latter part Light Airs & Inclinable to Calm. Hoisted Rear-Adm'l Sir J.B.Warren Flag ... came to with the Small Bower Anchor in 17 ft water ... fired 15 guns.'

They sailed straight away for England, the Admiral installed in comparative luxury in Cockburn's Great Cabin. We must assume that Warren had the decency to follow custom and offer Cockburn the small cabin on the larboard side (normally used as his dining room or an office) to sling his cot, and to share the Great Cabin with him.

The captain's journal becomes steadily briefer as the days go by;

> 'Tuesday December the 1st 1801. Strong Breezes & Squally ... St Agnes Lighthouse NNE 3 leagues ... 8 [pm] Lizard Lighthouse ENE 4 leagues. At 7 [am next day] the Bill of Portland NE 7 leagues. Several Sail in Sight.

> 'Wednesday the 2nd December 1801. Standing towards the Needles Point ... through the Needles at 3 ... running up towards Cowes ... let go the Small Bower and anchor'd at the Motherbank in 15 fms water ... saluted the Port Admiral with 15 guns.

> 'December the 13th, received 15 puncheons of beer...'

Discipline was hard to maintain. On Thursday 17th December, 18 dozen lashes, in all, were awarded for neglect, and Jas. Spellman got 1 dozen for 'Breaking his Liberty'. The following Tuesday a further 8 dozen were dealt out for neglect and disobedience, but by way of compensation the Clerk of the Check came on board at weekly intervals to pay the crew and, on Boxing day, 'agent onboard to award and pay prize money.' The last letter in Cockburn's 'letters out' file whilst commanding *la Minerve*, addressed to The Commissioners for Victualling his Majesty's Navy is, as ever, on practical matters;

La Minerve, Spithead, 13th Jany.1802

Gentlemen
There being on board His Majesty's Ship *La Minerve* under my Command, 21 Pipes of Wine, & as from her present state, it is not probable anything but Beer will be issued to her Crew for a considerable time, during which, it is very probable the said Wine may become sour, I have thought it right to appraise you hereof, that you may give such directions concerning its being returned into Store here, or otherwise as may appear to you best.'

Captain Cockburn's final accounts were approved, but he was relieved to receive a letter from the Office of Ordnance dated 5 February, whilst the ship was still at Spithead, about one item of expenditure which, if not approved, could have cost him dear;

'Sir

I am commanded by the Board of Ordnance to acknowledge the receipt of your letter dated the 27th of last Month, & to acquaint you, that in consequence of the predicament in which you was placed, in regard to the expenditure of Stores in the salute you fired in celebration of the Birth Day of His Royal Highne∫s, The Prince of Wales, as Commander of His Majesty's Ship *La Minerve* at Malta; and that as it appears there is no other objection to passing your accounts for that Ship, your certificate is likewise ordered to be granted.'

Minerve sailed for Deptford in February, where her powder and other stores were taken off. The paper-work continued to chase Cockburn, and the over-supply of wine seems to have remained a problem. However, Evan Napean, Secretary to the Board of Admiralty, himself wrote to Cockburn;

'Admiralty Office 17th Feby. 1802

Sir

Having laid before my Lords Commissioners of the Admiralty your Letter of the 16th Inst. acquainting me that the Ship you command is delayed paying off for want of permi∫sion to land some Wine which is on hand in her, I am commanded by their Lordships to acquaint you, that you should apply to the Victualling Office to obtain an Order from the Customs House for landing it, and that you are to send all the Men immediately to the Nore; having so done, pay the Ship off.'

After leaving Spithead the entries in the captain's log become even briefer than before:-

'Tuesday the 9th February 1802. Beating up the River Thames.

'Wednesday the 10th February... Beating up to Gravesend.

'Thursday the 11th February. Emp'd sending the Powder on Shore and getting the Guns out.

'Monday 15th of February 1802 [moored at Detpford] unbent the Sails and sent them to the Dockyard and strip'd the Ship to the lower Masts. Emp'd returning the Bosun's stores.

'Friday the 19th February 1802. Employ'd returning stores and provisions ... wash'd the 'tween decks.'

The final entry in the captain's journal, a particularly poignant one after all they had endured together for so long, simply reads;

'Saturday the 20th February 1802 ... sent the People away in the Gunboats to go to the Nore. At Sunset, the Men being all gone, hauled the pendant down.'

Samuel, along with many of his surviving shipmates, was said by *Minerve's* muster book to have been transferred to the *Zealand*, another captured ship kept as a floating barracks at the Nore. They were taken down to the Nore on HMS *Cracker* but he never officially entered *Zealand* – probably because there was a rapid scaling down of the Navy to save public money, now that peace had been declared, and there was now no job for him in the Navy.

Next day he was given passage in HMS *Diligence* 'for paſsage' as a 'supernumerary' and was entered in the purser's books 'For victuals only'. This was, in effect, his 'demob' transport to Yarmouth, which seems to have been his destination of choice, but whether or not he ever went home to his family in Devon we do not know; possibly not, as Yarmouth was an obvious starting off point for returning to his original career – a sailor in a merchant ship. On discharge from a ship, 'Shanks' Pony' was a man's normal mode of long distance transport back home – he walked.[127] Samuel arrived in Yarmouth Roads and was finally discharged on 1 March 1802 after a total of eight years and eight and a half months service.

La Minerve was not finally 'paid off' until April 1802, when the crew were paid. Samuel had already sent home a year's wages and was, on leaving the *Minerve*, able to send home a further £20 and was debited £4.4s.0d [£4.20] for 'Dead Men's Clothes' he had earlier bought.[128] Most of his contemporaries who had joined *Minerve* with him in 1795 were, by then, dead or had been invalided out of the ship, many of them having died in hospital at Ajaccio, on Corsica.

The Treaty of Amiens, establishing peace between Great Britain and France on what everyone in the Navy thought were totally dishonourable terms, was not finally signed until 27 March 1802. Many ships were paid off, and both officers and men found it impossible to find employment.

---

[127] Jacob Nagle describes how, pockets full of money, he and his comrades rode to London in a carriage; he also states that, each time his ship was 'paid off', all his money went in a few weeks only!

[128] A man dying at sea was given a traditional send-off, sewn up in his hammock (the last stitch through his nose, just to ensure he was not faking!) with a cannon ball at his feet to take him down to Davy Jones' Locker. If he died in action, his body was in the way so he was just bundled out of a gun port. His clothing and what few possessions he had were, by tradition, auctioned at the foot of the main mast as soon as possible afterwards. If he was popular, his mess-mates would bid far more than they were worth, as the proceeds were distributed to the next of kin.

St Vincent had thought highly of Hardy for taking *Mutine* and it was not long before he gained promotion as post captain. When the war resumed in 1803 Cockburn (Nelson's protégé, and his personal friend) naturally felt he was entitled to expect command of a '74' at least and had hoped for *Victory*. But his old friend and shipmate Hardy, who was junior to Cockburn, had the advantage of having served under Nelson at both the Nile and at Copenhagen. In the event it was therefore Hardy, rather than Cockburn, who was given command of *Victory*. It is amusing to speculate that, had *Victory* gone to Cockburn instead, school children might have learned of Nelson's dying words at Trafalgar, 'Kiss me, Cockburn.'

Instead of gaining command of *Victory*, Cockburn was sent on a special diplomatic mission to America in the frigate *Phaeton* (38). As with any popular captain, there was no shortage of volunteers for his new ship. Many of his old shipmates, his 'followers', were anxious to sign on with him again. But Samuel was not one of them.

After Waterloo in 1815 Napoleon surrendered to the allies on board *Bellerophon* – 'Bally Ruffian' as she was affectionately known – and it was decided that his final exile should be on the island of St Helena, in the South Atlantic. Rather fittingly, it was Cockburn (as captain of *Northumberland*) who was chosen to take him there. This time, there would be no escape.

Cockburn was able to establish a certain rapport with Napoleon on the nine weeks' voyage. To a certain extent he was able to continue this as Governor of St Helena during Napoleon's first six months of captivity there. He was said to be one of the few people not to be intimidated by him and had frequent discussions with him on the conduct and outcome of the war.

Later, Cockburn became an M.P. and, at the end of his career, was appointed Admiral of the Fleet. C. S. Forester, in his 'The Naval War of 1812' describes Sir George Cockburn as harsh and over-bearing, but no reason why is given; certainly he was not during his captaincy of *la Minerve*. After his death in 1853 the Langton baronetcy (motto '*Vigilans et Audax*' – vigilant and brave) passed to his brother William, the Dean of York, and thence to his nephew Alexander, the Lord Chief Justice. After that the title became extinct for want of a male heir. Cockburn was buried at Kensal Green, where Samuel's nephew Henry Blackmore, his wife and family lie buried.

But it is for his exploits in the unnecessary war of 1812 against America that

Cockburn is chiefly remembered.[129] Marching through deserted countryside with only a small combined force of soldiers, sailors and marines he found Washington undefended, and became famous as 'the man who burned the White House'. He also had the pleasure of demolishing the house of the proprietor of the local newspaper who had offended him by offering a reward of $500 for each of his ears!

Diadem's brief moment of glory came in August 1796 when *Captain* was sent southwards on other duties and Nelson temporarily transferred his flag onto *Diadem* but, as only a 64, she was not considered heavy enough for many of the duties of a 'ship of the line'.

La Minerve went to sea again when the war restarted, but was stranded at Cherbourg in July 1803, where she was recaptured[130] by the French ships *Chiffonne* and *Terrible*. She did not surrender without a fight – perhaps the bravest in her career in the British Navy. She was stranded, in a fog, on some huge stones which had been tipped into the sea as the first step towards the construction of a breakwater at Cherbourg. When the fog lifted it was found that they were well within range of the French batteries. But the captain, Jahlel Brenton;

> '…did not lose his head. He actually sent his boats in to cut out a French vessel which was close under the batteries, and which appeared suitable to carry out a bower anchor, while other boats harassed the French gunboats with their carronades … by ceaseless endeavors and magnificent seamanship they contrived to get the *Minerve* off the breakwater, and were getting her under way to sea, when the wind fell and left her becalmed. Before she could anchor the set of the tide carried her into the harbour and stranded her in a position where she could be pounded to pieces by the French batteries and, after putting up with it for an hour, Captain Brenton finally struck.'[131]

> 'A British sailor, who had both his legs shot off while the *Minerve* lay under the fire of the batteries, was carried to the cockpit. Waiting for his turn to be dressed, he heard the cheers of the crew on deck, and eagerly demanded what they meant. Being told the ship was off the shoal, and would soon be clear of the forts; "Then d—n the legs!" exclaimed the poor fellow, and taking his knife from his pocket, he cut the remaining muscles which attached them to

---

129 Pack, 'The Man who burned the White House'. Cockburn's voluminous papers (on which his book is largely based) were purchased by the Library of Congress in 1909. Microfilm copies are available in the Library of the National Maritime Museum at Greenwich and the Portsmouth City Library.
130 John Wetherell met two of her crew whilst a prisoner for 11 years in Givet prison in France.
131 The sea, its History and Romance, vol 3, by Bowen p90.

him, and joined in the cheers with the rest of his comrades. When the ship was taken, he was placed in the boat to be conveyed to the hospital; but determined not to outlive the loss of his liberty, he slackened his tourniquets, and bled to death.'[132]

The French had, in accordance with tradition, already named another ship '*Minerve*' when they lost her to *Dido* and *Lowestoft* in 1795, so she was promptly renamed *la Canonnière*. Even then her fighting days were still not over. On 21 April 1806, off the coast of South Africa, *Canonnière* was lying in wait for homeward bound convoys of British merchantmen, when eleven Indiamen hove into sight. They were guarded by two British men-of-war, *Tremendous* (74) and *Hindostan* (50). Ordering *Hindostan* to keep up her guard, *Tremendous* gave chase. The engagement started at 3.30pm with *Canonnière* firing her stern-chasers and *Tremendous* her bow-chasers. But by occasionally luffing up, *Canonnière* was able to bring her broadside to bear, causing considerable damage to *Tremendous's* sails and rigging. *Tremendous* managed to get ahead and was about to cross *Canonnière's* bows, giving her a raking shot, when a lucky salvo from *Canonnière* brought down her jib-stay and foretopsail and slings and also brought down her foretopsail yard. *Tremendous* then dropped rapidly astern. By then it was getting dark and that was effectively the end of the action.

A frigate had taken on, and beaten, a British seventy-four. But *Tremendous's* damage was easily put right, because her French adversary had, as always, fired high, and not a man was hurt, whereas *Canonnière* was badly damaged. A 32-pounder ball had just about severed her main mast, her mizzen mast and fore yard were badly injured and her two main anchors and a 36-pounder carronade were smashed. Seven men were killed and more than three times that number wounded.

Captain Bourayne's account was simple and factual, but a highly doctored version was printed in the 'Victoires et Conquètes'. Its readers were led to believe that *Tremendous* had been routed and made to flee, but *Canonnière* had been eager to board her, her crew shouting 'l'abordbage, l'abordbage.' She was yet again retaken by the Royal Navy in 1810. By now – stripped of her guns – she was called *Confiance*.[133] She was no longer in use as a naval ship (having been sold by the French navy into the merchant service in June 1809) and she was not taken back into the Royal Navy. The Royal Navy assumed that the useful life of even a British-built frigate was only about eleven years. She was, by then,

---

132 See Brenton, quoted verbatim in a much more detailed account than this, in 'James', vol III, p189.
133 Gardiner, 'The Heavy Frigate'.

completely worn out and was simply not worth the cost of a total rebuild.

The last French ship to carry *La Minerve's* illustrious name was a submarine, No.S647. On 27 January 1968 she was on exercises off Toulon when she failed to surface and sank in deep water 12 miles South South East of Cap Sicié with the loss of 52 lives.

Blanche was wrecked in 1799; it was her successor with the same name that fought under Nelson at the Battle of Copenhagen in 1801.

C.S.Forester, in one of his famous Hornblower books, said the *Berwick* was kept at anchor in the outer harbour of Toulon, where, to their frustration and annoyance, British officers and seamen on blockade duty could plainly see her each time they looked into the harbour there. *Berwick* fought on the French side, and was re-captured by the Royal Navy, at Trafalgar in 1805. She had been severely damaged. Like the remnants of both fleets, she was riding at anchor trying to weather the terrible storms that followed the battle, when the French prisoners on board bravely rose against their English captors and cut her anchor cables. She went onto the rocks and was lost, together with 200 men.[134]

Two further letters from Napoleon show that he had more in common with Nazi Germany than his British adversaries;

'To General Sault, Commanding the Camp at St. Omer.
La Malmaison, 23rd Pluviôse, Year XII
(13 February 1804)

Have the crews and gear of the fishing-boat which communicated with the English seized at once... Make the skipper speak ... if he would seem to hesitate, you can ... follow the custom as to men suspected of being spies, and squeeze his thumbs in the hammer of a musket.'

'To M Fouché, Minister of Police.
Milan, 10th Prairial, Year XIII.
(30th May 1805)

I have told you what you are to think of the reports the English are endeavouring to spread ... the newspapers must not be permitted to take a line favourable to Russia... A contrast must be drawn with the shameful position of the English. They must be compared to a besieged fortress...

Have caricatures made: An Englishman, purse in hand, entreating the various powers with money etc ... the huge care they are taking to gain time, by spreading false news ... prove its extreme importance.

---

134 James, 'The Naval History of Great Britain'.

Have it put about in Holland that news comes from Madeira that Villeneuve has fallen in with and captured an English convoy of one hundred sail, on its way to India.'

By 1802 Nelson's reputation was well known. Later, although still a national hero, the crowds flocking to see and cheer him where ever he went, he was often lampooned in cartoons and caricatures as arrogant, vain and full of self-glory. But what sort of man was he earlier on in his career, when Samuel sailed under him? Prince William (later the Duke of Clarence and then King William IV – 'the Sailor King') met him as a midshipman and had been recommended to learn all he could from Nelson, then recently appointed 'post captain'. He wrote that, as a seventeen year old midshipman, he had the watch on deck on Hood's flagship *Barfleur* at anchor off Staten Island;

> 'when captain Nelson … came in his barge alongside, who appeared to be the merest boy of a captain I have ever beheld; and his dress was worthy of attention. He had on a full-laced uniform; his lank unpowdered hair was tied in a stiff Hessian tail, of extraordinary length; the old-fashioned flaps of his waistcoat added to the general quaintness of his figure, and produced an appearance which particularly attracted my notice; for I had never seen anything like it before, nor could I imagine who he was, nor what he came about. My doubts were, however, removed when Lord Hood introduced me to him. There was something irresistibly pleasing in his address and conversation; and an enthusiasm, when speaking on professional subjects, that showed he was no common being.'

Although this story is intended to be about Samuel Blackmore and the life he and his shipmates led, we cannot leave Nelson without two later views of Nelson the man. First, a common sailor on *Royal Sovereign*, also called Samuel, wrote later;

> 'Our dear Admiral Nelson is killed! so we have paid pretty sharp for licking 'em. I never set eyes on him, for which I am very sorry and glad; for to be sure, I should like to have seen him – but then, all the men in our ship are such soft toads, they have done nothing but blast their eyes, and cry, ever since he was killed. God bless you! chaps that fought like the devil sit down and cry like a wench.'

Finally, his friend Dr Scott, *Victory's* chaplain, said;

> 'When I think, setting aside his heroism, what an affectionate, fascinating little fellow he was, how dignified and pure his mind, how kind and condescending his manners, I become stupid with grief for what we have lost.'

The only voice of public dissent, fortunately now forgotten by history, came from an unexpected quarter. Earl St.Vincent, whose earlier regard for Nelson had been fully reciprocated, did not attend the funeral. The prize money litigation with Nelson two years before had upset him deeply. He wrote, 'Lord Nelson's sole merit was animal courage. His private character was most disgraceful in every sense of the word'. When some of Nelson's private letters to her (which had been stolen) were published, he added that Emma Hamilton was 'a diabolical bitch'.[135]

---

[135] Nelson Dispatch, Jan 1992.

140

CHAPTER 9

When the fragile peace ended early in 1803, men were again urgently needed by the Navy to protect the Nation from Napoleon – more urgently than ever before – and none more than experienced seamen. The threat of invasion was even worse than before. Britain was now Napoleon's sole remaining adversary of any consequence. He had three armies totalling 167,000 men (to become the 'Grande Armée') encamped between Boulogne and Dunkirk and 2,343 invasion barges waiting to take them, together with all their horses and artillery, across to England. Only one problem prevented him from launching his promised invasion – the Royal Navy. When Samuel Blackmore had joined his first naval ship in 1793 there were around 45,000 men in the Navy. By the end of the war this had increased to 120,000 men.

We now lose sight of Samuel during the 'Peace of Amiens' of 1802, the resumption of the war by Napoleon the following year, the battle of Trafalgar and Nelson's death in 1805, Wellington's Peninsular War, Napoleon's defeat, imprisonment and escape from the island of Elba and the final victory at Waterloo in 1815. However we can still catch an indistinct glimpse of Samuel through all the gunsmoke of the second part of the war – correctly called the Napoleonic War.

It is known for certain that he neither rejoined *Minerve* nor followed Cockburn into *Phaeton*. A Certificate of Service was issued to him in June 1836, when he was 60. This suggests that he may have applied for a pension based on his years in the Navy, but he was never a pensioner at Greenwich. It may even explain why he had been 'reduced' from coxswain to A.B. in 1801. The certificate confirms that his career in the Navy started in *Diadem* as an A.B. in 1793, and that he was on *la Minerve* from August 1795 until February 1802. It also proves that Samuel never served in the Navy after that.

Why not? We can only conjecture. Perhaps he found some career where, thrown up on dry land at the ripe old age of 25, he had obtained a written 'protection' from the press-gangs who, again, roamed the streets seeking sailors to man his Majesty's ships more urgently than ever. However, protections were almost impossible to obtain in 1803. Sailors were again desperately needed, and written

*Side-lever engine by Napier from the paddle steamer 'Leven' (1828)
now at the Scottish Maritime Museum, Castle Street, Dumbarton*

'protections' held by experienced sailors were often ignored by the press-gangs.[136]

It is quite possible, therefore, that his absence from the Navy when the war was resumed in 1803 was due to injury, and that his injury prevented him from getting back into the only trade he knew. Did he have to look for some other sea-faring job where his disability was not a handicap? He was probably unemployed until the war started again but, if sufficiently recovered by then, would have had no difficulty in finding fresh employment in 1803.

Samuel's silver Naval General Service medal was not left specifically to anyone in his will, so it presumably remained in the family as a treasured heirloom for a generation or two and then passed through various 'junk shops' and the antique trade. It is recorded as first coming to light in a Brighton antique shop in 1972. Enquiries revealed that it had most recently been sold at auction in

---

[136] John Wetherell had a 'protection' as a carpenter on a north-country collier but, as he points out, this merely made him a more attractive catch to the press-gang that captured him. ('The Adventures of John Wetherell', edited by C.S. Forester.)

April 1994 for £8,400. Auctioned with it were two other items which are hard to explain. These were all in a specially made leather case. First, there was a bronze 'Arthur Davison' medal for the Battle of the Nile in 1798, a medal struck privately by Nelson's prize agent Arthur Davison and awarded to all who took part in the battle, gold for captains, silver for officers and bronze for seamen. It was naturally assumed to be his, but it cannot have been Samuel's, as he was not at the Nile; he was with *Minerve* in Portsmouth during her refit.

Secondly, there is the seal of the city of Calais referred to in the Blackmore family tradition. Maybe the explanation lies in the documentation included in the 1994 sale. The Nile medal is accompanied by a printed description of the medal and, attached to it, is a long-hand note on very fragile paper with a wax impression of the seal of Calais impressed on one corner;

> 'Medal of the Battle of the Nile –
> Samuel Blackmore Coxswain to Lord Nelson –
> Forfeited for insulting a French Officer at Calais. Returned with City Seal
>   on this paper.
> He was a prisoner of war in France for 16 years.'

The note was obviously not written by Samuel. He never was Nelson's Coxswain (perhaps the more the old salt told his story, the more it improved!) and, as the war resumed in 1803 and peace came with Napoleon's final defeat at Waterloo in 1815, he could not have been a prisoner for more than 12 years. Indeed, as Paris fell to the allies in March 1814, he would have been released after 11 years at the most – long enough!

If one supposes that Samuel went to sea again in a merchantman in 1802 or 1803, was captured yet again by the French before the press-gangs had the chance of catching him, and was held in France for the whole or a large portion of the second part of the war, it does at least explain where he was during that period and why he never served on a King's Ship again.

Pure romance, this; one likes to believe that Samuel was injured on *la Minerve*, but recovered sufficiently to rejoin John Company soon after his discharge from *Minerve* in 1802. The war re-started the following year and yet again, within a matter of months, he found himself in captivity, this time somewhere near Calais. Barbed wire had not yet been invented, so prisoners were usually kept in old walled fortresses. There was a line of these, now redundant thanks to Napoleon's re-drawing of the map of Europe, along France's former north-eastern boundary, including Verdun, Givet and Bitche. He may even have been in Givet prison, on the River Meuse some 225km south east of Calais, where

John Wetherell was held. One could expect that British prisoners held there would have been sent home via Calais, but John Wetherell's book says that, as the war was coming to an end and the allies were crossing the French borders in their drive for Paris, the prisoners did not stay at Givet but were marched to and fro all over France.

Wetherell mentions meeting three men in Givet prison from *la Minerve*, but he was not referring to Samuel – they had been on her when she was re-captured by the French in 1803. He also describes how, the swollen Meuse having swept away the bridge, the prison authorities enlisted the help of the seamen prisoners to build a pontoon bridge to get Napoleon and his entourage across on his way to one of his campaigns. Was Samuel one of the men who were involved?

A complicating factor is that Samuel christened his first child, a son, at Dover in 1812, which suggests that he was back in this country again and married his wife in 1811 or earlier. If he was held prisoner, how did he return before the war ended, or at least before 1813 when the allies pushed Napoleon back into France after his disaster at Moscow? Again, a faint but somewhat unlikely clue. A book on prisoners[137] contains a list of those few men whose records have been found and a note as to what became of them – 'died', 'escaped', 'exchanged', and so on. Once again, chance plays a hand for there, large as life, is Samuel Blackmore's name, listed as a midshipman. Was this the same man? Probably not; Blackmore was not a particularly rare name in the South West, and Samuel was a popular Christian name. Besides, to have been promoted midshipman would hardly have been likely for a man who, although he attained petty officer rating as a coxswain, had never become a warrant officer – bosun, or gunner, for example. But the chances of an exchange were greater for officers than common seaman. So did he somehow manage to impersonate a midshipman in order to enhance his chances of being sent home, and succeed? Unlikely – but how else did he get back to Dover, marry and produce a son before the allies came in 1813 or 1814 to free him?

As to the Nile medal and the Calais seal, did he make friends with another seaman in the prison camp and have the medal given to him or, more likely, acquire it by way of trade for something he was able to sell, such as alcohol or tobacco? And did the French give him his seal (a simple wax impression on paper) when he was freed? The story about Samuel insulting a French officer sounds entirely likely, knowing the Blackmore temperament! He would naturally have treasured the Nile medal (no matter how he came by it) and,

---

137 'Napoleon and his British Captives' by Michael Lewis, 1962.

'The Elfin' *despatch steamer*

when the NGS medal with its three clasps was presented to him in 1848, he would have kept them both together, along with the wax Calais seal. After his death, it would be natural for his family to assume that the medals were both, rightfully, his and someone wrote the longhand note to record their origins for the sake of posterity.

Minerve was said[138] to have been involved in Egypt in 1801, where Sir Sidney Smith commanded a Naval Brigade of 1,000 men, assisting the 6,000 soldiers under Abercromby. However, *Minerve* is not listed as one of the ships that participated in the landings in March 1801. Her Captain's Journal, for the entire period from the landings in March 1801 until the final surrender of Alexandria on 2 September, makes no mention of the ship being moored up or at anchor at Aboukir Bay (where the British Fleet lay), Alexandria or anywhere else in Egypt. Besides, Lord Keith, like any other Commander-in-Chief in the Mediterranean, was desperately short of frigates.

With all due respect to Douglas-Morris it is improbable that Keith would have taken a frigate's crew out of their ship to fight on shore with Sir Sidney Smith's Naval Brigade. Had he been there, Samuel would have been entitled to a medal for 'Egypt'. Rather than have a fourth clasp to his naval medal, this would have

---

[138] 1984 Auction sale catalogue and the accompanying research notes of Capt K J Douglas-Morris, the foremost naval history researcher of the day and also an expert on naval medals and author of the standard tome on the NGS medal. One hates to question an acknowledged expert, particularly one who is no longer alive to defend himself but, in the absence of any such suggestion in *la Minerve*'s log, one wonders on what evidence this is based. We must also question his reference to Samuel being 'prest' from the East Indiaman *Imperial* (see Chapter 1 above), as the East India Company papers at the British Library show no ship of that name in the East India Company's fleet at or around that time.

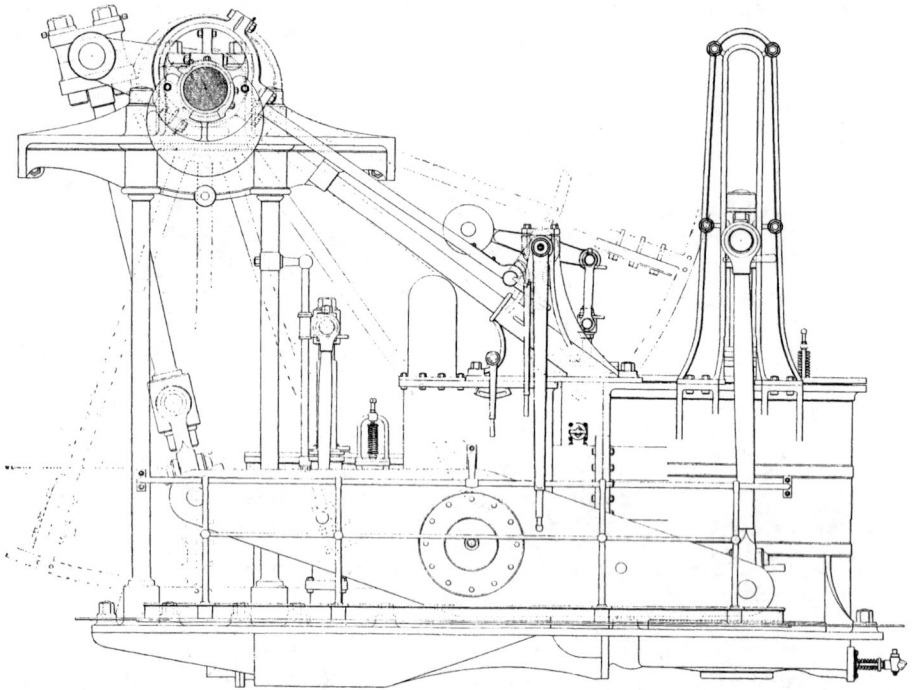

A side-lever engine.

been the corresponding army version, the Military General Service Medal. Like the Naval General Service medal, it was in all other cases awarded in 1848 to applicants who sent in their applications the year before. However, the Royal Warrant for this particular action, only added to the list later, was not announced in the London Gazette until 1850. Even if he had been entitled to it, Samuel by this time was getting very old and probably never heard of it.

The Blackmore family tradition that Samuel was captain of a cross-Channel 'packet boat' seemed to imply that he had been on a Post Office vessel, so a visit to the Post Office archives at Mount Pleasant was the obvious next step. Surprisingly, they have a mass of papers going back into the 18th century. There Samuel was found again, after the war, living in Dover.

Samuel's prize money, probably quite a considerable sum for those days, stood him in good stead. He was able to buy himself a freehold house at Black Ditch (which, hardly surprisingly! was later renamed Princes Street) in Dover where he lived with his wife, son and daughters. He was shown on the Poll Lists as there from 1815 onwards.

Being a freeholder, he applied for and was awarded the Freedom of the City of Dover in 1820 (giving him the right to vote in parliamentary and local elections) together with Thomas Mercer, another 'mariner'. Was he a friend, and did he give his Nile medal to Samuel? Mercer does not feature in the NGS list for the Nile; there is a Thomas Mercer, but his clasp is for Syria – a generation later. Our Thomas Mercer could have been at the Nile and got his Arthur Davison medal, but not survived long enough to apply for his NGS medal.

The Post Office archives at Mount Pleasant include records of appointments of captains of Royal Mail packet boats. No Blackmore captains are mentioned, but the Post Office archives contain some fascinating papers about the first steam-driven paddle steamers that replaced the sailing ships in the Post Office service. A problem encountered by the Post Office was how to construct paddle wheels large enough to transmit the full power of two 40 horse-power Boulton and Watt engines, whilst maintaining the sea-worthy qualities of the ship. The senior Post Office captain was very anxious; the engineers advocated a longer, heavier ship, but the civil servants at Post Office head-quarters wanted a shorter, lighter and above all cheaper ship with engines of only 30 horse-power. The correspondence does not say how the full power from the smaller engines in a smaller vessel could be transmitted by smaller paddle wheels!

The Post Office were also concerned that the need to take fare-paying passengers and freight, as well as the Royal Mail, to make the service pay, meant that the Crown was becoming an 'entrepreneur', a function that still worries some.

After Trafalgar, the Navy sometimes had difficulty in accepting new ideas. Sir William Symonds, Surveyor to the Navy, wrote in 1837;

> 'Even if the propeller had the power of propelling a vessel it would be found altogether useless in practice, because of the power being applied in the stern it would be impossible to make the vessel steer'.

Admiral Sir George Cockburn, who served on the Admiralty Board from 1818-30 and again from 1841-46, was in favour of steam propulsion. He supported the idea of screw propulsion, too, and was behind the successful trials of *Rattler*, a screw-driven vessel, against two paddle-steamers. But Nelson, a generation earlier, is said to have had other views. When the American, Robert Fulton, suggested the use of steam to drive a ship, he is reported (on what doubtful authority[139] one does not know) to have replied;

> 'What, Sir, you would make a ship sail against the wind and currents by lighting a bonfire under her decks? I pray you excuse me. I have no time for such nonsense.'

Although there is no evidence that Samuel had ever been appointed as a Post Office captain, there are two 'Minutes' from the Post Office agent at Dover that mention him. According to Post Office records, the Royal Mail packet *Crusader* (one of the first paddle steamers[140] on the Dover to Calais run) was grounded on the beach outside Dover harbour in a storm on the night of 21 October 1833. Other than Post Office records, the only information obtained about the incident is an entry dated 22 October 1833 in Lloyd's List;[141]

> 'Dover. 21st [October 1833]
>
> The *Crusader* Steam Packet, in coming for the harbor [sic] this afternoon from Ramsgate, got behind the North Pier, and remains in a precarious situation.'

Samuel was injured whilst helping to get her off. It must have been a terrible night, for the seas broke right over her as she lay stranded and washed sand and gravel down into her engine room. The formal minutes read;

> '14. <u>Dover Blackmore and Hammond. Officers of Crusader.</u>
>
> 15 November 1833. I regret to see these Casualties amongst our Officers as well as the veſsels themselves at Dover as the injuries were received in discharge of duty. I presume your Grace will readily authorise the payment of wages and Medical Attendance whilst under cure.
>
> Approved. RICHMOND.
>
> <u>Blackmore – Mailman of Crusader – Surgeons Bill.</u>
>
> 6th March 1834 – For the Postmaster General. Your Grace authorised Medical Attendance in the Case. The Charge appears very moderate recollecting the severity of the injury and the length of time the Case has been under care.
>
> Approved. RICHMOND.'

---

[139] Nelson kept himself informed on new developments (vaccination, for example) and must have heard about the trials of the tug-boat, the *Charlotte Dundas*, in 1802. Steam had also been used by Richard Trevithick in a successful road locomotive in 1801, and Thomas Newcomen's beam engines had been in regular use in mines since about 1712. Nelson could not have been unaware of these applications of steam power.

[140] One of the first steam packet boats, not a Post Office one, was employed from Brighton to Dieppe as early as 1823, and features in hazy outline in Turner's painting of the Chain Pier at Brighton.

[141] At the Guildhall Reference Library, London, which now keeps the Lloyd's archives.

The first two Post Office steam-driven packet boats, both paddle-steamers of course, were built in 1821 under Admiralty supervision. They were made of wood, painted black with a broad white stripe down the side, and were first used on the Dover-Calais run in 1826. There were two cabins, one for six women in two-tier bunks and another for fourteen men. *Crusader* was one of the smallest at only 108 tons. Her length was 100 ft, her beam 16 ft and her displacement 108 tons. She was built in 1827, probably in an Admiralty yard, as the cross-Channel packet service, when it resumed in 1815 (with sailing ships, of course) was taken over by the Admiralty.

She had two 'side lever' engines which, with the paddle-wheels and funnels (one, with its boiler, ahead of the engines, and the other aft of them) were mounted between the two masts. It seems, however, that *Crusader* was eventually engined, not by Boulton & Watt, but by Maudsley & Sons, Bolton. Her two engines gave her 60 hp, which drove her at 11 knots, and the passage from Dover to Calais took just under three hours with a favourable wind.

As one of the early paddle steamers, *Crusader* would have been designed to rely on sail whenever possible, in order to save coal and provide a cover against breakdown. It is highly doubtful that she had a 'bridge' in the current sense, as she was flush decked, but she could well have had a bridge or catwalk spanning between the two paddle boxes. An Illustrated London News print of the 'despatch steamer *Elfin*' in about 1850 shows a small paddle steamer which seems to have been about the same size as *Crusader*. Her helm is right aft, and the helmsman cannot see ahead because of the paddle-boxes and the engine housing amidships, so another seaman stands on top of the engine housing and, by means of hand signals, instructs him where to steer.

The packet service between Dover and Calais was run on a reciprocal basis, with boats simultaneously crossing from each side. Then, as now, the French knew how to be difficult. There was neither explanation nor apology if the French packet boat was disgracefully late but, if *Crusader* or one of the other packet boats on the Calais run was only five minutes late, after a crossing in strong winds with mountainous seas, there was always an instant formal complaint. The postal authorities in both countries had agreed minimum fares for passengers and rates for horses, carriages and freight, but the French quite openly charged as little as one third of the agreed rates, in order to divert trade from the English packet boats to theirs. The French boats would frequently leave a few minutes earlier than the agreed sailing times, in order to attract passengers. The Postmaster General's decision on all these issues was to continue to play it by the book and not to lodge a formal counter-complaint, as that would only lead to yet further difficulties.

In 1836 the Admiralty considered that the Post Office were not looking after their vessels properly and were not keeping them up to date, so they were taken over by the Royal Navy who promptly changed their names.[142] Post Office internal minutes show that, like other packets at the time, *Crusader's* name was carefully selected from a list of possibles, all chosen by the Post Office to convey a dynamic, modern, go-ahead image. On taking her over, the Admiralty renamed her *Charon*; wasn't that the name of the ferry-man who, in Greek mythology, conveyed the dead over the River Styx to their final destinations?

Other Post Office minutes on the subject of the October 1833 storm damage record the regret of the Duke of Richmond (Postmaster General) at the number of injuries and the need to repair the 'vefsel' speedily. The Duke of Richmond was mindful that 'wrecking' was in the blood of Englishmen; the local people could just as easily have stripped *Crusader* bare. He therefore wanted to know the steps taken to reward those inhabitants of Dover who had rendered assistance. He said it was essential to establish the precedent of rewarding them; the Post Office might not be so lucky next time there was an accident!

The Court of Enquiry, acquitting Captain Lyne of negligence, was held only five days later. Unfortunately, luck ran out here. The 'Dover Telegraph' would have given more information, but copies are only available as from the beginning of the following month. However, internal Post office minutes relate the tale sufficiently. *Crusader* went onto the beach an hour before high tide in frightful weather conditions, the *Ferret* and other Post office vessels came to her aid and two other packet vessels suffered severe damage in the storm. Quite a few people were injured. The *Salamander* had to be taken off the Ostend service to help out on the Calais run.

The Duke of Richmond had just approved a recommendation that all the Post office boats on the Ostend run should be fitted with four-inch guns; one would love to know why! A clerk in the Post Office at London wrote on 23 October in a memorandum to the Duke of Richmond;

> 'It is very gratifying to see that the *Crusader* has received such very trifling damage – I never had any fear for the Vefsel, provided they could once get

---

[142] 'Paddle Warships' by D K Brown. Maber's book says 'The Admiralty was responsible for the carriage of the over-seas mails from 1823 until 1860, when control was returned to the Post Office.' The Admiralty were responsible for mail to more distant places, but this is plainly wrong so far as the Channel mail was concerned.

*"The London to Paris Mail Coach, at the High Street Canterbury Stage, Christmas 1830",
by Leslie Simpson F.R.S.A.*

her off, as her bottom is a solid maſs of Timber, and she would lie fair on the shingle – my only apprehension has been for the Machinery, which if they are not very careful will be exposed to much injury from the Sand and gravel which has got into it. I have written to the Agent to desire that the Engines may have a complete overhaul before she is suffered to go to sea, and to imploy [sic] competent Smiths to aſsist…'

So Samuel was not, after all, the captain[143] of the good ship *Crusader*, nor even her first officer, but only her 'Mailman'. To get any responsible job at the Post Office (even delivering letters) it was necessary to put up a substantial 'bond', to be of good conduct, and also produce a letter of recommendation from some noteworthy person. Retired naval officers were frequently approached for references by ex-sailors who had served under them and Samuel could well have written to one of the officers he had served under, possibly even Sir George Cockburn himself, to obtain one. This could possibly be taken to confirm that,

---

[143] The four captains on the Calais run each received a salary of £400 a year, plus 2 per cent. of all passenger and other receipts over £10,000 p.a. divided between them.

in 1801, he had not been reduced from Coxswain and re-rated A.B. for some terrible act of misconduct, but that he had been injured.

Samuel was still living at 3 Princes Street, Dover with his wife Margaret, their surviving daughters and a servant when the 1851 census was taken. His son, two of his daughters and his wife all died before him. He himself died on 30 September 1854 and was buried with his wife in what is now called Cowgate Cemetery, Dover.

One does not know what a 'Mailman' was, or what Samuel's duties on *Crusader* were. As an 'Officer' of the Post Office, he was probably responsible for seeing to the loading and off-loading of Her Majesty's Royal Mail, and for guarding it with his life until it was safely delivered to the authorities in Calais. Whilst on the voyage across, however, could he relax and – is it just possible – go up on deck or even on to the bridge, as Blackmore family tradition had it, 'clad as to his feet in carpet slippers'?

Josiah Nisbet, Nelson's step-son who had been a midshipman under him, at one time had a house at Exmouth. He died in Paris in 1830. Within a few years four of his children also died there. Lady Nelson, who also lived in Exmouth, arranged for their bodies to be brought back there and buried in the parish church graveyard up the hill at Littleham.

The Blackmore connection with the Nelson family continued, for Samuel Blackmore's brother, John, as the Parish Clerk was responsible for the funeral arrangements. The wheeled bier, used to carry the bodies up to Littleham, is on display in the Exmouth Museum. Lady Nelson herself died and was also buried at Littleham in 1831, only just a few yards away from the group of Blackmore family graves where John and his wife lie buried. Also buried nearby are the remains of Nancy Perriam who joined her husband in *Orion* and served as a powder monkey at both St Vincent and Aboukir Bay. She died in 1865, apparently aged 97.[144]

The family's connection with the sea also continued. A local newspaper records this about one of Samuel's distant Exmouth cousins;

> "2 July 1857. Smuggling. William Mutter and Charles Blackmore were committed to the Devon County Gaol on Monday for safe custody on a charge of illegally landing 45 tubs of brandy under the cliffs between Exmouth and Budleigh Salterton. They will be brought up at Exmouth on Saturday.

---

[144] Exmouth Journal, 28 September 2000.

Lady Nelson's grave at Littleham, Exmouth, Devon.

9 July 1857. Smuggling. We stated last week that two men named William Mutters and Charles Blackmore had been apprehended on a charge of smuggling. They were brought up before W.Cole Esq., and Rev.T.Boles, magistrates, at Exmouth last Saturday....The evidence was to the effect that at about 2 o'clock on Monday morning week Richard Jago, Coast Guardsman belonging to Exmouth, was on his beat at Straight Point and observed a boat a little distance from the shore. A Coast Guardsman from Budleigh Salterton, named William Wagg, soon joined him, and both descended to the beach. The two men, Mutters and Blackmore, hid themselves from the Preventive men, but the latter made a search and, having found them, immediately fired an alarm for assistance from Budleigh Salterton, when Mr Prawle and his men came over. They found 41 tubs and 4 flagons and other articles. The Bench found the Prisoners guilty and fined them £700 or six months imprisonment. They were committed to gaol."

Charles seems to have got himself into rather bad company, as it appears that the Mutters family were professional smugglers, and had been so for several generations.

This extract is from a leather-bound book which my grandfather won as a prize at school. I am including it for no better reason than that I thought it might amuse other rowing and ex-rowing men, including Matthew Pinsent, who is probably my very distant cousin. Samuel Blackmore's nephew married a farmer's daughter whose mother's maiden name was Pinsent, a well-known Devon family, as was his. His family became respected lawyers in Birmingham. By coincidence my old firm in Leeds, Simpson Curtis, merged with Pinsents in Birmingham shortly after I retired and is now called Pinsent Curtis Biddle.

FROM 'MEMOIR OF A BROTHER',

By Thomas Hughes, author of *Tom Brown's Schooldays*.

> At this time ... rowing was at rather a discount at Oxford. For several years Cambridge had had their own way with the dark blues, notably in this very year of 1841. But a radical reformer had just appeared at Oxford, whose influence has lasted to the present day, and to whom the substitution of the long stroke with the sharp catch at the beginning (now universally accepted as the only true form) for the short digging 'waterman's' stroke, as it used to be called, is chiefly due. This was Fletcher Menzies, then captain of the University College boat... He had selected my brother, though a freshman, and had taken him frequently down the river behind himself in a pair-oar. The first result of this instruction was, that my brother won the University pair-oar race, pulling stroke to another freshman of his own college.
>
> In Michaelmas Term, 1841, it became clear ... that the opposition was triumphant. F.Menzies was elected captain of the O.U.B.C., and chose my brother as his No.7... The race against Cambridge was then rowed in the summer, and over the six-mile course, between Westminster and Putney bridges. The weather was intensely hot.
>
> It [1842] was the last race ever rowed by the Universities over the six-mile course... My brother unluckily lost his straw hat at the start, and the intense heat on his head caused him terrible distress. The boats were almost abreast... This was the crisis of the race. As the boats separated, each taking its own side, Egan, the Cambridge coxswain, called on his crew: Shadwell, the Oxford coxswain, heard him, and called on his own men; and when the boats came in sight of each other again from behind the lighters, Oxford was well ahead. But my brother was getting faint from the effects of the sun on his head, when Shadwell reminded him of the slice of lemon which was placed in each man's thwart. He snatched it up, and at the same time F. Menzies took off his own hat and gave it to him; and, when the boat shot under Putney Bridge with a clear lead, he was quite himself again.

The following year, Oxford beat a Cambridge crew at Henley with only seven men rowing in the boat.

THIS BOOK IS BEING SOLD EXCLUSIVELY FOR THE BENEFIT OF CHARITIES

Some copies of this book are being sold for the benefit of Holy Trinity Church, Little Ouseburn, Yorkshire, the author's local church. Others are being sold by the Nelson Society and the HMS Trincomalee Trust (both charities) through their respective sales channels for their own benefit.

A victim of bowel cancer himself, Anthony Blackmore has arranged for all the remaining copies to be sold for the benefit of BEATING BOWEL CANCER (charity no: 1063614), a charity set up by the author's fellow bowel cancer victim, the former BBC Watchdog presenter, Lynn Faulds Wood.

As he is carrying all the production and printing costs himself, EVERY PENNY goes to charity, not just any profit earned from the book or even only a few pennies per copy as royalty.

Bowel cancer kills so many people. It is now Britain's second-worst cancer killer, second only to lung cancer but, if caught in time, it need not be fatal. It is, unfortunately, a subject that too many people do not like to talk about – least of all with their doctors.

The first step towards reducing the number of unnecessary deaths from bowel cancer, and catch it early, is to raise awareness in the minds of members of the public.

Thank you for buying this book.

NOTE TO 2nd IMPRESSION

In place of Beating Bowel Cancer (for whom sales of the 1st impression raised over £2,400) the major beneficiary for sales of this 2nd impression will be LYNN'S BOWEL CANCER CHARITY, a new charity being set up by Lynn Faulds Wood.